LANCASTER
AT WAR:3

The Grand Old Lady

As I walked through the meadow I saw her,
Aloof with nose in the air;
Ignoring the people who went passing by
Disdaining their curious stare.
Her legs, so delicate, seemed too frail
For the body they supported;
She had shared her life, with a great many men
Excitement and danger she courted.
But the days of her youth are now over
And it's true, she is well past her prime
'Just an old Lancaster bomber',
Once cherished by crews
That she brought safely back, every time.

Ken Moore

Supreme and Proud

We had no common bond
Save that of youth;
No shared ambition,
Except to venture and survive.
Until, aloft within that roaring fuselage,
Each dependent on the others,
We found in war's intensity
Good cause to say with pride in later years
To those who chronicled the great events,
We flew in Lancasters.

Philip A. Nicholson

Cover caption: *Limping Home* by Robert Taylor.   The colour illustration on the jacket is a detail from Robert Taylor's original painting *Limping Home*. Depicted is a Lancaster bomber, damaged by flak and enemy fighters, struggling to maintain height and reach the English coast.
Reproduced by kind permission of the Military Gallery

1   The Dusk will Always Belong to Them. The silence is uncanny. Not for *you* the sights and sounds of a busy airport with holidaymakers hurrying here, scurrying there, hoping to catch the sun in distant places. Before your vision lies a brooding expanse of mystery, a land of awesome contact with the past, its overpowering atmosphere setting your imagination in full cry. There is a sense of laughter and of sorrow as long gone airmen of the past, passing before you in limitless procession, can be heard hailing their names above the moaning of the trees. It is like walking in an endless graveyard, silent enough to maintain the illusion. So, too, do the unheard sounds of Merlins fill the dusk as 'Moose' and 'Ghost' Squadron Lancasters once more come home to roost. As the last Lanc is lost to view in the darkness now beginning to flood the aerodrome, you sense it is time to go. Suddenly you feel spent and exhausted.

Here a discarded Halifax sits it out at Middleton St George circa April/May 1944 as a No 419 ('Moose') Squadron RCAF Lanc X is about to alight on return from a training flight during the unit's conversion period. These days (1983) this one-time two-squadron No 6 Group base serves the North-East as a busy civil airport under the name Tees-Side.   *Public Archives of Canada*

LANCASTER
AT WAR:3

Mike Garbett and Brian Goulding

GUILD PUBLISHING
LONDON

First published 1984

This edition published 1984 by Book Club
Associates, by arrangement with Ian Allan Ltd

© M. Garbett & B. Goulding 1984

Printed in the United Kingdom by
Ian Allan Printing Ltd

2

2 It's up to You Now Skip'. Your first positive indication of
approaching battle would be the distinctive mutter of Merlins. All
around the field each sleeping giant you were responsible for would
be awakening while you would still have your head down, affording
pleasure from a lie-in, or perhaps easing your way through a
leisurely late breakfast. Just when to amble down to dispersal would
depend, of course, what Group had planned for you; when you had
landed from your last trip and slipped beneath the blankets; how
much patching, stripping and replacing your ground crew had been
forced to effect. The factors were many. Whatever the reason, your
kite would be in the capable hands of your fitters and riggers,
armourers and electricians, instrument bashers, radar mechs and
their breed. You depended on them totally; on their eyes which
watched for the slightest trickle of oil from a vital pipe joint; on
their ears that strained for any falter in the note of a Merlin; on
their hands that tightened every nut and screw with such loving
care. Though they stayed behind, their thoughts went with you on
every trip.

Their job done, a line of erks stand aside to watch 'PO:H' of
No 467 Squadron RAAF being run-up against the chocks at
Bottesford, autumn 1943. *RAAF Official*

Contents

3

3 Days Without Number. For six long years Sundays lost their meaning. Come to think of it, Saturdays, too, lost their identity. Month in, month out, every day was the same. Your sole reason for living was to get the crews in the air, to keep them pounding the enemy, give the Axis no rest. Time meant little. Did it matter what the world about you was doing? Surely, all that mattered was the weather, the flying . . . and the bright oasis of nights in town, and each all-too-short 48 or 72-hour pass as and when. You accepted that no glamour surrounded changing the plugs of a Merlin or oiling a Lanc's Brownings. It was a job, no more than that, and you did not resent the boys with wings — lads most of 'em, just like you

— all their leaves, their gongs. What use were they if death awaited, so often resulted! They did not court a press who boosted their deeds, their exploits; nor did they seek, yet fully deserved, the handshakes and free drinks an admiring public thrust upon them. You, at least, *knew* you were going home one day . . . .

Another day unfolds at Binbrook, circa December 1943, as fitters and riggers of the largely Aussie-manned No 460 Squadron remove soaking covers from cockpit and turret Perspex, tyres and engines . . . as yet the only audible sounds of action coming from cawing rooks in distant woods. *F. E. Harper Collection*

6

Foreword

Air Marshal Sir Harold 'Mick' Martin
KCB, DSO and BAR, DFC and Two BARS, AFC, RAF (Rtd).

In this their volume 3 on the *Lancaster at War*, the co-authors have compounded a remarkable anthology of pictures, prose and poetry.

Much of the material has come from the hearts and memorabilia of many airmen whose connection, in one way or another, with Lancasters has left them with the feeling that each aircraft had a character and soul of its own.

Readers who flew, or serviced this famous aircraft will become totally immersed as they turn the pages and re-live days and scenes long forgotten, or recall acts of human endeavour and sacrifice of which there were so many. The stuff that victory is made of.

Those readers who were too young for such experiences will be fascinated as they are guided through with clarity vivid slices of Lancaster history.

My own crew had a pleasant introduction to the 'Lanc' through the Manchester in which we did the three 1,000 Bomber Raids of 1942. The Manchester was a splendid aircraft but a frustrating engine development problem left it on the side track, an act of destiny perhaps which led Roy Chadwick and his team under Roy Dobson quickly to evolve the 'Lanc' installed with Merlin engines. No instrument of war made a greater contribution to Nazi defeat than the 'Lanc' when handed over to the Commander in Chief of Bomber Command, MRAF Sir Arthur Harris, Bt.

Our crew was sent ranging far and wide in our 'Lanc' P for Popsy as she was named. Although on occasions the airframe was badly damaged and crew members hit by the Air Defences, she never failed to get back.

I have not flown a 'Lanc' for 39 years and feel it would be of interest if Sqn Ldr Anderson who demonstrates the Lancaster for the Battle of Britain and Bomber Command Memorial flight would recount his sensations of flying this war winning aircraft today.

January 1984

Preface

When the idea of *Lancaster at War* was first conceived in 1969, little did we think that some 14 years later, not only would the 'At War' series, to which it gave birth, be still going strong, but also that we would be asked to produce a Volume 3 on our beloved Lanc. The original *Lancaster at War* was published in 1970 and Volume 2 in November 1979; both are still in print! What a tribute to the aircraft! This volume has been woven round that magic word: L-A-N-C-A-S-T-E-R. The format is different; the message much the same.

Affection for the Lancaster, and wave of nostalgia for the period seems to have heightened with the passing of the years — perhaps a natural process as men age, standards appear to fall, and as the supreme sacrifices of men are transcended by new philosophies and ambitions. The Lancaster represented a shining period, when everyone in the free world worked and pulled together against the forces of evil.

Yet the widespread and obvious feelings of awe and pride in the Lancaster, and what it represented and achieved in the hands of determined young volunteers, are to be found not only amongst those who were directly involved with bomber operations; but — even more significantly — with the younger generation too, the sons and grandchildren. It is not easy to understand, but is there for all to experience at any air show at which the RAF's last flying Lancaster appears.

Without exception, the crowd 'freezes' at the sound of her four Merlins. Many tears are unashamedly shed; hairs rise on the back of necks; men stand inches taller, as she growls by, canopy and turrets glinting briefly, every inch of her somehow in perfect harmony of motion. Surely no other aircraft in the world can evoke quite such emotion and respect.

When our humble efforts at research began over 30 years ago, we decided at a very early stage to concentrate our attention on the men who flew, maintained and operated the Lanc in whatever capacity (not forgetting the ladies, of course). In those early days, they were young people, to whom the memory of war was still fresh — so fresh, they wanted to forget it. Persuading them to part with photographs, to relate stories, reveal inner feelings or state opinions, was not the easiest of tasks. There is now a much greater willingness to do so, and to assist authors.

Regrettably, but irrevocably, all who were on Lancasters are nearing, or actually into, retirement. Even more regrettably, many are no longer with us, the strain of fighting a war having caught up. Let there be no doubt as to the part they played. Fortunately many of the still-young-at-heart survivors are to be found these days at the regular round of reunions and association meetings which have become established, and a large number of former individual crews have been reunited for the first time since their end-of-tour goodbyes. It is good to see, too, the large numbers of Commonwealth airmen revisiting their old stations, looking-up former colleagues and friends of 35-40 years ago.

Without the contributions made to our research by ex-air and groundcrews, our six previous books would hardly have been feasible. As it is, we wish to record our appreciation to all those who have assisted us over the years. They must now number into four figures, so to name but a few would be impossible. However, we must mention specially in this volume, the following:

Few are more qualified to write our foreword than Air Marshal Sir Harold B. (Mick) Martin, KCB, DSO and Bar, DFC and two Bars, AFC. An Australian by birth, his energy and ability know no bounds and, following a distinguished career in the Royal Air Force, he is an active as ever — at the time of life when most are resigned to retirement — as a roving salesman/businessman with a leading British aviation concern. A legend in his own lifetime. Sqn Ldr CSM Anderson readily took up Mick's challenge of writing a 'final word' for our book. As OC the Battle of Britain Memorial Flight, he has what many would consider to be best job in the Royal Air Force. This may well be true, but believe us when we say there is far more to it than flying the Lancaster, in company with Hurricane and Spitfire on a punishing round of annual displays. Thanks Scott — your willing staff too — for a memorable day one September, a day which saw two buffs realise the long-cherished dream of flying in a Lancaster *together*.

Three contributors who put their considerable talents and time at our disposal are Philip Nicholson, Harry Smith and Eric Chapman. Philip, one-time wireless operator with No 115 Squadron and now a headmaster, has submitted poetry to various periodicals both in the UK and USA, and won wide acclaim. The poems he composed for us stem from wartime experiences vividly recalled almost 40 years after the events. Harry, who also served as a wireless operator in No 3 Group (No 186 Squadron), led an equally active life until he died suddenly in April 1983. Besides being head of an arts and crafts department in a Grammar school, and tutor in adult education, he was an accomplished artist; a member of The Royal Institute of Painters in Water Colours, The Free Painters and Sculptors, etc, his work will continue to be well known in the Potteries and beyond. A delightful man, we are the poorer for his passing, yet we see no reason why an inspired collection of silhouettes should not become a treasured heirloom in the years to come. Eric Chapman willingly stepped in to complete the range of silhouettes begun by Harry. A self-employed commercial artist for more years than he cares to remember, Eric can lay claim to a connection with every operational Lancaster: as a young man he worked in the design office of the Aldis Company.

No less talented is Ken Moore, composer of poem 'The Grand Old Lady', and former air gunner long since grounded as a stores controller. Ken, like Philip Nicholson a gifted poet, finds little difficulty recalling his aircrew days in No 3 Group, and his many poems are well known to No 75 Squadron veterans, again in contact with their British cousins, and who have journeyed from New Zealand in recent years on pilgrimages to renew friendships and revisit old haunts.

For the donation of the peom 'Anywhere But Where I Am' we are indebted to Harold Bryans, a No 630 Squadron bomb aimer who spent almost a year as a POW after his crew was shot down on only its second operation. Like us, Harold feels sure that whoever penned this quite outstanding composition (possibly a fellow POW?) will not object to its publication. Would that we knew his identity.

Restless since retiring from British Airways, our old friend Joe Nutt, wartime flight engineer with Nos 207 and 97 Squadrons, enjoyed perusing old records to tie-up loose ends and check our facts. Thanks, too, go to his able helper Ray Priest. As ever Bob Roberts performed wonders with fading prints, and Cyril Parrish has continued to work unstintingly on our behalf in the darkroom. Eric Chapman's spouse, Lilian, typed the bulk of the manuscript, ably backed up by Mavis Warner. All showed commendable tolerance and understanding.

More old friends closely associated with this book include Harold (Barney) Brookes, the most generous of men, for his untiring efforts on behalf of kindred ground crew (Aussies and others who served with No 463 Squadron RAAF may remember him); Jim Carpenter, driving force behind the Midlands Area Bomber Command reunions, as well as being active with the Air Gunners Association, for many favours. Jim was a rear gunner with No 192 Squadron in 100 Group and still cannot understand why his beloved Halifax receives such scant recognition! Stan Hanson (navigator, 207) and Gerry Murphy (bomb aimer, 101), both contributors to *Lanc at War 2* represent a host of ex-aircrew who spent countless hours in discussion, proof-reading, offering advice and suggestions.

One advantage of being an enthusiast-cum-historian is the opportunity of forming lasting friendships with the men who did the deeds we study and write about; men typified by Cliff Hill DFM (rear gunner, 35) and Wg Cdr Jimmy Bennett DFC and Bar (pilot and CO, 550), ever ready to offer a meal or bed for the night. We salute Beryl and Joan, too — indeed all wives — for *their* invaluable contribution and support. Charles Cuthill DFC (pilot, 149), Bert Pearson DFC (navigator, 12) and Al Mercer (Canadian bomb aimer, 431) figure among the many who generously allowed access to their private memoirs. Bert also provided the delightful cartoon which accompanies these acknowledgements.

Of the many stories written and taped for us over the years, it has been possible to select but a few. The choice is always difficult. Our thanks to the authors of those chosen for this volume, and for their response to our painstaking quest for accuracy and attention to detail: Cliff Allen, Frank Bone, Stan Bridgman, George Calvert, Bob Gross DFC, Ray Harris DFC, Tom Matthews DFM, Ted Robbins.

Illustrating the Lancaster in her many facets has not been easy. It must be remembered that for much of her life she operated at night, whilst cameras and the taking of snapshots were actively discouraged. Even so, many men 'begged, borrowed or stole' in order to take home some visual reminders of what many referred to affectionately as their mis-spent youth. Thankfully, too, there were men who, either through foresight or the collecting mania, risked much to gather together remarkable records of their war service. E. Darwin Evans was an instrument mech at Binbrook and Ludford Magna (No 460 Squadron and 14 Base). He happened to possess a good camera, and — more importantly — the foresight and determination to record many intimate, and at the time seemingly routine aspects of life on the stations, becoming accepted eventually as a semi-official photographer. His efforts must be almost unique, and the results have proved a source of inspiration in the preparation of Volumes 2 and 3 in which many of his pictures have been used. Our sincere thanks Darwin. Other substantial contributions have been made by similarly inspired photography buffs Mike Bachinski DFC (Canadian flight engineer, 431), Les Bartlett DFM (bomb aimer, 50) and Vic Redfern (fitter, 101). To them and others of their ilk, our undying gratitude.

We are grateful to all those who entrusted to us their flying logbooks, photographs, and other priceless material, enabling us to accumulate a vast library on the Lancaster and all its facets; and to maintain our tradition of using mostly non-official pictures to illustrate our books. Whilst some of these may not always be of the best quality, we feel they nevertheless serve to illustrate so well the atmosphere and moods of an unforgettable era. Few of the photographs used in our books will have been published before, a feature of which we are proud.

We have endeavoured to convey the real feelings, opinions, and emotions of the time, not only pictorially, but by using the language in which the stories and accounts have been related to us: euphemisms and nomenclature, jargon and slang, much of it conceived in the war, still used by many today, particularly in the services. We hope its use will bring back many memories and will not be construed as presumptuous; nor give the mistaken impression that 'we were there'. It is an attempt to be fully authentic out of deference to those who *were* there. It was *their* language. We, as mere authors, can never know quite what those young men endured on our behalves.

Mike Garbett and Brian Goulding

Glossary

AA	Anti-aircraft
A&AEE	Aircraft & Armament Experimental Establishment
AGLT	Air Gun Laying Turret (radar-controlled)
Airborne Cigar	Listening/Jamming device
Aldis	Signalling lamp manufactured by the Aldis Company
Ammo	Ammunition
AMO	Air Ministry Order
AOC	Air Officer Commanding
AP	Air Publication
ASR	Air-Sea Rescue
AVM	Air Vice-Marshal
BABS/ Eureka	Homing device
Bash	A boozy night in town. Generally having a good time
Bind	Depressing job/situation
Bod	Real person. Short for body
Boomerang	An aircraft that returns without dropping its bombs. Also referred to as an early return
Bull	Nonsense. Nonsensical orders
Bumph	Printed papers, orders. Vulgarly said to be fit only for toilet paper!
Cans	Incendiary clusters mounted in boxes/cans
CAT AC	Category minor damage; repairable on unit/ site
CAT E	Category beyond repair; a write-off
Circuits and bumps	Flights around the aerodrome and landings performed over and over again by way of practice
Civvy street	Civilian life
Cookie	4,000lb blast bomb
CO	Commanding Officer
Cpl	Corporal
Dak'	American Douglas Dakota transport aircraft
DFC	Distinguished Flying Cross
DFM	Distinguished Flying Medal
DI	Daily Inspection
Dipso	Well under the influence of alcohol. Taken from dipsomaniac
DRO	Daily Routine Order
DSO	Distinguished Service Order
EFTS	Elementary Flying Training School
Erk	An aircraftman. Any airman below corporal rank
ETA	Estimated time of arrival
Fizzer	Disciplinary charge; a charge report
F700	An aircraft's log book
'Flight'	Flight Sergeant
Flip	Joy-ride
Flt Lt	Flight Lieutenant
Flg Off	Flying Officer
Flt Sgt	Flight Sergeant
Fort'	American Boeing B-17 Fortress heavy bomber
FTR	Failed to return
Gear	Any equipment but especially an airman's kit, clothes
Gee	Navigation aid
Gen	Reliable information
G-H	Navigation/bombing aid
Gong	Medal, decoration
Goose-neck	Paraffin emergency flare with a long neck
GP	General purpose
Greaser	Extension of a 'three-pointer'. A good landing when all three wheels touch down together
gremlins	Mythical mischievous genus of creature, specially invented by the RAF as the cause of anything that goes wrong
Groupie	Group Captain
H_2S	Navigation/bombing aid
Hairy-Do	Occurrence that has serious consequences or just escapes them. Also known as a Shaky-Do or Dicey-Do
Hallybag	Handley Page Halifax heavy bomber
HCU	Heavy Conversion Unit
I/C	In charge
i/c	Inter-comm'
IFF	Identification Friend or Foe
ITW	Initial Training Wing
Kipper Kites	Any aircraft of Coastal Command detailed for convoy or fishing fleet escort duty
LAC	Leading Aircraftman
LFS	Lancaster Finishing School
Lib'	American Consolidated B-24 Liberator heavy bomber
Lt	Lieutenant
Lobbing in	Originally a landing for emergency reason but extended to cover any unexpected landing
MF/DF	Medium frequency/Direction finding
Monica	Fighter warning device
MP	Military Policeman
MT	Motor Transport

MU	Maintenance Unit	'Sarg'	Sergeant
NAAFI	Navy, Army and Air Force Institutes	Scrub	To eliminate, to wash out
NCO	Non-Commissioned Officer	'second	Pilot flying with a seasoned crew for
NFT	Night Flying Test	dickey'	experience before taking his own crew on
Nissen	Hut of an easily-erected type. Originated by		operations
	Canadian mining engineer Lt Col P. N. Nissen	Snag	Defect
	DSO. Semi-circular, made of corrugated iron	sprog	Originally any airman under training but
Oboe	Navigation/bombing aid		extended to anyone raw or inexperienced
OC	Officer Commanding	Sqn Ldr	Squadron Leader
OCU	Operational Conversion Unit	Sgt	Sergeant
OTU	Operational Training Unit	S of TT	School of Technical Training
Oxbox	Airspeed Oxford trainer	Tiger	De Havilland Tiger Moth trainer
'paddle		Tiger Force	Bomber group scheduled to go to Okinawa in
steamer'	Lancaster fitted with paddle blade propellers		order to bomb Japanese homeland in
PFF	Path Finder Force		conjunction with the Americans
pit	Bed	USAAF	United States Army Air Force
Plt Off	Pilot Officer	u/s	Unserviceable
POW	Prisoner of War	u/t	Under training
Prang	To damage, destroy, wreck	VC	Victoria Cross
PT	Physical training	VHF	Very high frequency
QDM	Magnetic course to steer with zero wind in	WAAF	Women's Auxiliary Air Force
	degrees and time	Wangle	A fiddle in a mild sort of way. By-passing the
RAAF	Royal Australian Air Force		system
RAF	Royal Air Force	'Window'	Strips of foil to confuse enemy radar
RCAF	Royal Canadian Air Force	Wingco	Wing Commander
RN	Royal Navy	Wg Cdr	Wing Commander
RNZAF	Royal New Zealand Air Force	WO	Warrant Officer
R/T	Radio/Telephone	W/op	Wireless operator
Sally Ann	Salvation Army	W/T	Wireless/Telephone
SBA	Standard beam approach	Y-run	Cross-country training flight using H_2S radar

FULL LOAD - SHORT RUNWAY

Three Times Down but Not Out

Bob Gross

The role played by aircrew in the transition from medium to heavy bombers was of tremendous significance. Fortunately many of the pilots were, at that stage, men of considerable experience, who had been flying in either the RAF or RAF Volunteer Reserve since before the war. They and their crews would find themselves having to absorb the intricacies of two new types within the space of only a few weeks, with barely a pause in the operational commitment. The pressure on everyone to get the new types hurried into service was enormous, adding considerably to the levels of stress under which they were living and working. Whether you were aircrew, groundcrew, office personnel or a storesman, you all had a part to play.

No 44 (Rhodesia) Squadron was scheduled to convert from Hampdens to Manchesters late in 1941; but with production of the Manchester ceasing suddenly, the squadron found itself instead taking the first Lancasters to come off the production line, the initial batch arriving on Christmas Eve. What a present!

The squadron was fortunate in that a number of its newly appointed senior officers had been directly involved in the Lancaster's proving and service acceptance flying programme at Boscombe Down for several months previously, thus bringing with them a unique nucleus of experience on the new 'wonder bomber', as it was described.

In contrast, No 97 (Straits Settlements) Squadron was operating spasmodically with Manchesters when selected as the second unit to receive Lancasters. A signal was received at Coningsby advising that some of the new aircraft were ready for collection, so several of No 97's more experienced pilots flew over to Woodford in a Manchester. Each was given a 15-minute demonstration flight in a Lancaster by an AVRO test or production pilot, before flying a brand new specimen back to Coningsby, with only their regular co-pilots as crew.

Unlike the Manchester, the Lancs were not fitted with dual controls, so the newly qualified Lancaster pilots, with all of one hour's four-engined experience, then had the task of converting the rest of the squadron's pilots to the new type. For the 'students', it was a question of looking over the other's shoulder for a couple of circuits before climbing into the seat for a go at it themselves.

There were no Lancasters to spare at that stage for issue to training units, though as more became available, each squadron allocated one or two machines to its own conversion flight. It was to be several months before some of the Lancs from the early batches which survived long enough, passed to the newly forming Heavy Conversion Units, which helped to quicken the flow of new crews as the Lancaster force expanded.

It took the first Lanc squadrons (Nos 44 and 97) about two months to work up to operational status, and on 17 April 1942 they were to operate together on the spectacular, but very costly Augsburg raid, following which the Lancaster was officially announed to the public for the first time.

It was intended that the Manchesters should pass out of No 5 Group to the squadrons which were to form the nucleus of the new Canadian Group. An example was No 420 (RCAF) Squadron, which briefly converted from Hampdens to Manchesters at Waddington in May/June 1942. In the event, the Canadians rejected the Manchester; they wanted something better for their money, and instead opted for the Halifax which was then available in some quantity.

The aircrew viewpoint of the transitional phase is well illustrated in this account of an air gunner, Sgt R. G. W. (Bob) Gross:

'After flying eight sorties, as under gunner with No 83 Squadron on Hampdens, I was transferred to Coningsby where I joined No 97 Squadron, which was endeavouring to cope with the many problems of the Avro Manchester, the colossal failure which, when modified into the Lancaster, became the finest bombing aircraft of the war. On 28 September 1941 I teamed up with Sgt Gordon Hartley and his crew who also had some operational experience, and after the usual familiarisation flights we were briefed for our first Manchester raid on 20 October 1941, our target being Bremen. The reputation of the Manchester was such that a member of a Manchester squadron was pitied rather than admired; yet to me, after the freezing experiences of a Hampden and the uncomfortable positions in which the under gunner had to operate, the giant size of the Manchester exuded an air of confidence, albeit sometimes mistaken. Two

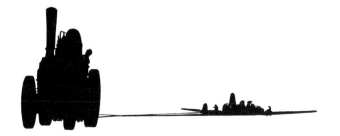

belt-fed Brownings were also a decided improvement on two Vickers gas-operated guns with drum feed, although the entrance to the mid-upper turret and its lack of space was a decided disadvantage.

'R5783, "OF-V", became airborne at 18.20 and set course for Bremen, carrying a heavy load of 1,000lb GP bombs. The raid itself was rather uneventful: moderate searchlight activity, a certain amount of flak on the approach, and heavy fire over the target. Although some of this was fairly close, we did not think we had received any hits and set course for home.

'Shortly before our ETA English coast, the second pilot reported that the fuel situation was becoming critical, either due to the extreme thirst of the Vulture engines, which seemed unlikely after about six hours in the air, or possibly from loss of fuel due to a petrol tank being holed by AA fire.

'Our W/op transmitted an SOS and we flew on. Suddenly it was reported that we were over land and our chances looked brighter. However, Gordon ordered us to prepare for a crash-landing and the rear gunner and myself left our turrets and took up our positions at the main spar. The engines spluttered and stopped and the nose went down as the pilot glided in. Not much time can have elapsed before we hit, as we were only flying at about 1,000ft when the engines packed up, but it seemed hours.

'Memories flooded through my mind, but, strangely enough, no fear. I had, of course, endured a similar situation in a Hampden when we crash-landed safely some two months before, and in neither case had the subject of baling out been raised, although both situations had arisen in the middle of the night, hardly the best time to crash-land with no power!

'Suddenly we hit, tail first, and bounced, then hit again, and water began pouring into the fuselage. As we had been over land when I left my turret, the possibility of landing on water had not entered my head, and a ditching was a more unpleasant situation than a crash-landing.

'The Manchester soon stopped and began to settle as we ploughed through the rising water to the top escape hatch. The observer was already out on the starboard wing and he shouted that there was grass and the plane couldn't sink. He jumped on to the "grass" which was floating on the water and was immediately up to his waist, and frantically climbing back on the wing.

'The dinghy had not ejected but the plane appeared steady enough; the water was not rising any more, so we assessed our position. Everything outside seemed quiet, and very dark. We couldn't see land so had no idea of our position. It was decided to fire off recognition cartridges from our Very pistol, which was duly done, giving a very pleasant pyrotechnic display in assorted colours. Through this light we could see that the shore line was not very far away (by the light of the Very cartridges we actually saw the barbed wire defences), making us feel rather more content.

'Our signals disturbed no-one to our great surprise as we had expected this part of England to be well protected against possible invasion, but everyone slept on, except us.

'We were feeling cold and wet, knowing that we would now be considered "missing in action"; but having no other option, we decided to wait for daylight.

'At first light Gordon, the captain, stated he was wading ashore, the water level having dropped as the tide receded. So off he went, while we considered the possibilities of him being blown up by mines, or other anti-invasion devices. However, nothing happened and he reached the shore, climbed up an embankment, waved and disappeared from view. (We realised, at first light, we were inside the barbed wire defences and that they were not between us and the shore as we originally thought). Just on the point of deciding we had waited long enough, we heard noises from over the embankment where Gordon had disappeared, so we decided to abandon the aircraft and investigate.

'We waded ashore, climbed the bank and there saw some distance away a man and his horse working the land. To the right we saw a small house out of which appeared a female figure. We started towards her, and must have startled her more than somewhat, but we shouted out that we were English and within five minutes were in front of the fire in her house with a hot drink and some bread and dripping to stave off the pangs.

'We enquired about our signals which she said she'd seen but thought they were from ships out at sea, and hadn't unduly bothered about them. Neither had anyone else if they had been seen. We asked about mines and other defences, and found out that there were none, apart from barbed wire fences; also no troops in the immediate vicinity. So much for our "fortress England"!

'Eventually came the sound of a vehicle and on going outside we discovered that Gordon had found a telephone, organised transport and was back to pick us up. We duly thanked our hostess, gave her what money we had in our pockets (only loose change, I'm afraid) and returned to base, wet, bedraggled, tired, but quite happy, especially to find that even though our SOS had not been received we had not yet been listed as missing though the ditching had been at 00.30hrs off Friskney, near Boston.

'Following our experiences of 20 October our crew only made three more operational sorties up to the end of November, due to both weather and aircraft problems; but in December the pattern changed and the squadron embarked on a programme of formation flying and air firing training, culminating, as expected, in a daylight raid on Brest where the *Scharnhorst* and *Gneisenau* were berthed.

'Fortunately our crew was not selected for the operation on which we lost the Squadron Commander (Wg Cdr Balsdon) when his aircraft crashed whilst attempting a landing after being damaged by flak.

'Over the Christmas period we continued with training for a further daylight formation raid on the same target, even flying on Christmas Day, to the disgust of all concerned, and were then informed that we would have an early call on Boxing Day morning for briefing for the raid.

'Fortunately, we were never called and the raid was abandoned.

'Instead another crazy idea was implemented.

'Ourselves and another crew were sent off to practise dive bombing on the local bombing range. This was a hair-raising experience. The Manchester was a heavy bomber, not designed for dive bombing techniques, and Gordon had to

4, 5 To be Continued in Our Next . . . With the tide out, Manchester I R5783 'OF:V' looks like a stranded whale on the mud flats near Friskney. Recovery was by No 58 MU, Newton, using a locally hired traction engine. Surely those barbed-wire defences had more effect holding the natives in, rather than keep out a determined enemy! *Both: C. S. Waterfall Collection*

develop his own tactics as we went along. I thought the aircraft was going to fall apart when we made our dive and pulled out, and sat in the fuselage, near my parachute, in case of trouble.

'We gradually improved, thanks to a home-made bomb sight, and attained a reasonable accuracy, but knowing the strength of the defences at Brest, the idea of two Manchesters getting away with dive bombing the two battleships, and returning to talk about it, seemed remote.

'On 6 January the raid was on, and then postponed.

'On 8 January it was on again and at 14.50 we took off in L7459, "OF-V", a Manchester I, for a night-flying test, carrying a load of practice bombs for a last rehearsal.

'I was in my usual take-off position, sitting in the fuselage under the mid-upper turret, near the flare chute, when Gordon opened up the engines and we commenced take-off.

'We had reached a considerable speed when I noticed that smoke was seeping through from the bomb bay. Realising something was wrong I called the captain. Within seconds the interior of the fuselage was a mass of foul smoke, but the aircraft still kept going. We became airborne, not for long, and hit the ground again very hard indeed. Again we were in the air, but the engines were cut back and I realised we were committed to a crash. Directly in front our line of take-off were No 106 Squadron dispersal huts and their Hampden aircraft, and also the camp sewage farm.

'We hit again, the undercarriage collapsed; I presume Gordon had selected wheels-up, and ploughed on completely blind. The aircraft stopped suddenly, the sound of metal breaking and distorting also stopped. I felt a bang against the back of my right thigh and decided to leave. I staggered to the rear door, which I managed to open, and rushed out, coughing and retching to find the remainder of the crew, appearing from various escape hatches, spluttering away but all apparently unhurt. We were quickly taken to sick quarters where we were given oxygen to clear our system and discharged within a couple of hours, with two or three days off flying, and an extra ration of milk in case of any damage caused by the smoke from the practise bomb.

'We returned next day to the scene and found that we had, after our first bounce, floated over the sewage farm and landed in a small field. The aircraft had skidded on until it embedded its nose in the embankment of the canal. I had a large weal on the back of my thigh, and remembering the knock on it went inside the fuselage to investigate. I found the starboard propeller had been ripped off and impaled in the ground. As the aircraft skidded forward one blade had sliced through the fuselage like a can opener. It had stopped exactly by the flare chute where I'd been standing. Six inches more would have seen me off for good! The Manchester was a complete write-off.

'March 1942 and I still hadn't flown an operation since 30 November. The squadron, however, had re-equipped with Lancasters, which, even though various teething troubles were being experienced, was, so far as we were concerned, a vast improvement on the Manchester. The mid-upper turret, though still difficult to crawl into, was considerably larger and more comfortable.

'We had also left the permanent aerodrome at Coningsby for the new aerodrome at Woodhall Spa with the austerity of wartime temporary accommodation. So once again we had the familiar problem of finding out about the new aeroplane, mainly for the pilots: four engines instead of two; swing on taking off, the opposite way to that in a Manchester. However, all was well and I was anticipating my next sortie, which apart from being my first in a Lancaster, would be my 13th. I, like many others, was superstitious and four months was a long time to wait.

'On 23 March we took up L7574 for an NFT, only to find when coming in to land that the undercarriage warning lights read one red, one green. No amount of manoeuvring, or use of emergency drills could alter the situation. The duty pilot in Control (Dave Maltby, later to become famous with the Dambusters) suggested to Gordon that the trouble could be electrical, and that the wheels were probably locked down, so we came in to land. Fortunately he was correct, the fault was electrical and we landed safely and reported it, the aircraft being made u/s.

'We were briefed for a fire raid on Essen but at the last minute, due to a poor weather forecast, the raid was cancelled.

'However, as our crew lacked experience on Lancasters we were instructed to do a cross-country but were told to be back by 9pm as the weather would be closing in after that time.

'Transport drove us out to the aircraft, R5486, where we were informed that it was still bombed-up. Gordon said that our instructions were quite clear and he was prepared to take the aircraft as it was. To this the sergeant replied that it would make a grand bonfire if anything went wrong (as you will realise, after R5783 and L7459 and other minor problems, we had achieved some notoriety!).

'We accordingly became airborne at 19.35 and flew our cross-country course as ordered, in Lancaster B1 R5486, "OF-P".

'We arrived back at base in good time, so we thought, but because of bad weather, we couldn't find it; nor could we contact it by either R/T or W/T. We also had a new radar aid, Gee, but this also didn't do us any good. We were therefore in the very unpleasant situation of flying around over Lincolnshire, fully loaded with incendiaries and unable either to see the ground or make any wireless contact whatsoever.

'Fortunately for us we received aid from an unexpected quarter. Searchlight beams some distance away beckoned us and directed us northwards leading us to an illuminated runway, which on contacting by R/T after circling, we discovered to be Finningley.

'Feeling very relieved we commenced our landing approach, when again the undercarriage lights started playing tricks, one red, one green. Emergency drills were carried out, but the lights stayed as they were, and Gordon was compelled to overshoot and circle the landing area, which was grass, there being no concrete runway at Finningley at that time. Because of the previous occurrences only a few hours earlier, we assumed the fault was most likely electrical, but came in to land with utmost caution. Once again I was sitting on the step over the bomb doors under my turret.

'All seemed well as we touched down and rolled on. Then I noticed the aircraft appeared to be tilting to port; there was a flash of flame and suddenly the port engines and wing were on fire. Gordon managed to stop the aircraft with the tip of the port wing on the ground, the starboard wing pointed upwards at a crazy angle. Flames were all over the port side and I dashed to the rear exit, on the starboard side, and jumped out.

'As usual, the crew were appearing from various exits until only Gordon was missing, but we found him, still in his seat, in full control, switching off engines, petrol, and with one half of the aircraft in flames and a full load of incendiaries underneath.

'He made his exit from the escape hatch and joined us on the ground where a brief check showed the usual "no damage" to any of the crew, apart from a ricked ankle by one crew member who climbed on to the starboard wing, which, being tilted upwards was rather higher from the ground than he anticipated when he jumped off.

'A roar of engines signalled the arrival of the fire brigade and other vehicles. By this time the fuselage was well ablaze and the firefighters didn't make much impression.

'When we advised them that we were fully loaded with incendiaries, they decided to call it a day, jumped aboard the fire engine and were away!

'We were left watching the display as the incendiaries started to explode, throwing flames high into the air, when we realised that our position was rather exposed, so we made our way to the watch office to make our explanations and apologise for putting their aerodrome out of action for the night.

'We examined the remains next morning; virtually nothing one could recognise, and we were then driven back to Woodhall Spa to receive on arrival many ribald and sarcastic comments on our latest exploit (or escapade).'

Following these incidents the crew settled down to something like a routine tour and completed a further 12 trips together before splitting up, Bob Gross doing two more ops as a spare bod before himself being declared tour expired. He was to complete a second tour with No 9 Squadron from Bardney in 1944.

Sadly, Bob passed away in 1978.

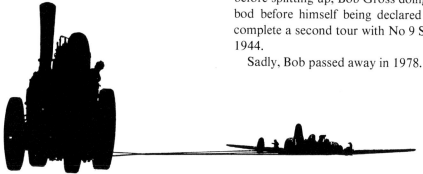

L Lineage

WHAT IS A LANCASTER?

Is there anybody here who doesn't know what a Lancaster is?

Maybe you're too busy on one bit of it to stop and consider what the whole affair amounts to.

It's a regiment.

It's an artillery unit and an A.A. post.

It's a reconnaissance outfit.

It's a transmitting station.

It's a battery of heavy howitzers.

It's the most potent destructor of enemy morale.

ONE LANCASTER IS ALL THESE THINGS.

HOW MUCH COULD SEVEN BRITISH SOLDIERS DO IF THEY LANDED ALONE IN GERMANY?

WHAT CHANCE WOULD A DETACHMENT OF LIGHT ARTILLERY HAVE AGAINST THE DEFENCES OF A GERMAN CITY?

HOW MANY AGENTS WOULD WE NEED TO GET FACTS ABOUT A RAID ON GERMANY?

HOW LONG COULD WE MAINTAIN A TRANSMITTING STATION ON ENEMY TERRITORY?

HOW LONG WOULD IT TAKE A BATTERY OF THE HEAVIEST ORDNANCE TO REDUCE 300 ACRES OF AN ENEMY TOWN TO PULP?

SEVEN MEN OVER GERMANY CAN DO MORE THAN A REGIMENT ON IT.

ONE LANCASTER'S GUNS CAN KNOCK DOWN MORE ENEMY AIRCRAFT THAN A SCORE OF A.A. POSTS.

ONE LANCASTER'S OBSERVER CAN REPORT MORE OF A RAID THAN FIFTY SECRET AGENTS.

ONE LANCASTER'S WIRELESS IS A DIRECT PRIORITY LINE TO THE BATTLE FRONT.

ONE LANCASTER CAN DO MORE DAMAGE IN SIXTY SECONDS THAN A BATTERY OF HEAVIES IN MONTHS OF BLOOD AND SWEAT.

ONE LANCASTER OVER FRITZ'S HEAD IS WORTH ALL THE PROPAGANDA IN FIVE CONTINENTS.

Seven soldiers wouldn't scare him much. But a handful of British airmen with a nestful of British H.E. bombs can make a million Nazis shake in their ersatz shoes and wish their War was over.

Some day we may send men in thousands with bayonets, guns, cannons, tanks, mortars, shells, scouts, signals, dispatch-riders, transport, stores, kitchens, and hospitals.

That will be to finish the job; to put the final polish on it for good and all.

But we're on the job now. We want to save time, labour and precious lives.

What's the machine that will do that AS NOTHING ELSE CAN in the whole works—in the whole Universe, Land, Sea and Air, at this present hour?

You've got the answer in your own two hands,—

YOUR LANCASTER

7 True Worth. How many of you remember a two-sided flimsy handed out at OTU, HCU, wherever? You believed every word of it at the time! *A. Price Collection*

8-11 Some did . . . Some didn't. Were you in No 5 Group during the early years of trial and endeavour, long before the Second Front became a reality? If so, you surely have a Manchester prang to relate. As often as they stayed up, they came down, and it surprises you not when you learn that almost as many Manchesters *fell down* as were shot down! You took to carrying a tooth brush and other essentials before you departed on even the allegedly simplest of cross-country hops for you never knew where you might end up. And you — and your ground crews too — suffered continuous taunts and jibes, from those who still flew Hampdens. Did you not end up behind the wire before your time, there to send the half-expected coded message which told your seniors back home the 'how and why' of your demise? You found the Manchester pleasant enough when her Vultures behaved themselves, but all too frequently they did not and you spent as much time watching your engines and gauges for signs of trouble as you did doing the job you were sent up to perform. You cast many a longing eye on the four-motor Stirling, then the 'star of the show'; the Halifax, too,

promised much. You were not to know that all those boring endurance trials helped pave the way for those who followed you and flew the mighty Lancaster.

Illustrated are some typical Manchesters . . . with and without their Vultures running. (8) No 97 (Straits Settlements) Squadron's L7459 'OF:N' in sorry attitude following an abortive NFT, 8 January 1942. Sgt Gordon Hartley and crew hit trouble taking off (laden with practice bombs) and finished up on a bank in a field beyond Coningsby. That they avoided No 106 Squadron's dispersals, and floated over the camp sewage farm was quite remarkable. Talk about fate? This was the crew's second Manchester prang within three months and they would write-off one of 97's first Lancs before they were through (see Bob Gross's account). *R. A. Fletcher*

(9) Triple-finned 'EM:X' up from Waddington in 1941 is a reminder that No 207 Squadron started it all back in November 1940 and persevered with the type until converting to Lancs during January 1942. *P. C. Birch*

(10 and 11) L7521 — one of a surprising number of the 200 Manchesters produced which recorded more than 300 hours flying. Before crashing on Waddington's perimeter, 5 September 1942, when with No 50 Squadron Con Flight, she had served No 61 Squadron well enough (as 'QR:W'). *P. C. Birch; N. N. Wilkie*

12-14 The Basic Breed. From the operating angle, the Lancasters you flew did not change all that much in three years of war. Whether yours was an original Avro-built BI of 1942 with Merlin XXs, or a 1945 Canadian BX with Packard-Merlins 224s, you still stalled with undercarriage and flaps down at 92mph indicated air speed when your weight was 50,000lb . . . knew your standard fuel tankage was 2,154gal . . . had the same barely adequate escape hatches and rear door for a fast exit as and when. OK, so they swapped a few things round — and sometimes made life more difficult, like blocking the fuselage when moving the mid-upper forward and exchanging the hydraulically operated Frazer-Nash FN50 with its .303in Brownings, for an electrically activated Martin job mounting two .50s. The heavier armament was long overdue but your gunner found his new turret constricting, difficult to enter — and get out of in a hurry. And you still don't understand why a Lanc thus equipped, fitted with Merlin 24s and built by Austin Motors should be designated a BVII, not a BI! After all didn't Victory Aircraft in Canada produce Lancs with Merlin 38s or 224s and still call them BXs whether equipped with Frazer-Nash or Martin mid-upper? To add to the confusion Austins even turned out a batch of 50 Lancs with the Martin turret and dubbed them BI (BVII Interim)! Allowing for enemy interference, you found it no problem to be taking a BIII to Berlin one night, a BI to Stettin the next. That your own spanking new 'paddle steamer' was in for repair and you were down to take the veteran, long overdue for retirement, getting slower every trip, you took in your stride. If you had any hesitation at all it was that you as skipper and engineer did your vital actions correctly when starting up and taking off . . . remembering what happened when you forgot you were handling a BIII or BX with Packards and Bendix-Stromberg carburettors!

Forget airframe numbers and squadron markings and it's virtually impossible to tell which marks of Lancaster are illustrated here. (12) BI W4158, among the first Lancs received by No 9 Squadron when it re-equipped at Waddington during August 1942. Initially fitted with Merlin XXs, she at one time had Merlin 28s outboard when engines were in temporary shortage at No 622 Squadron, Mildenhall early in 1944. As she later passed to No 3 LFS, Feltwell it is probable she reverted to true BI standard. (Struck off charge December 1945.) *L. F. Farey*

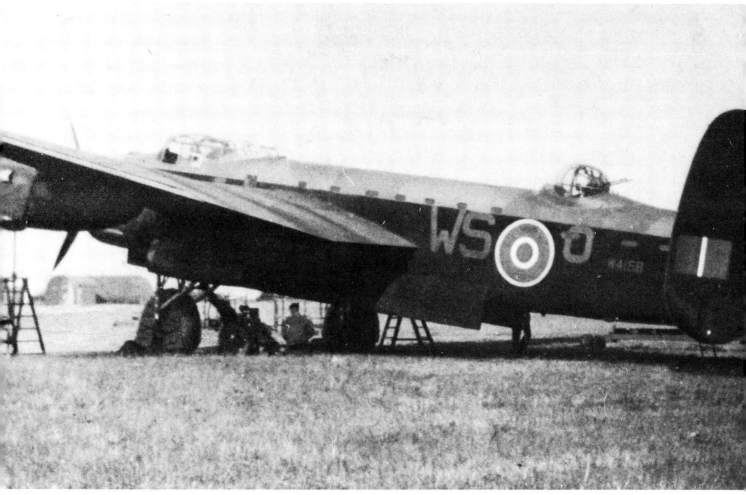

12

(13) BI (BVII Interim) NX565 with No 12 Squadron, Wickenby in 1945 looks no different to a true BVII, even a BX. (She went to No 15 MU, Wroughton in July 1946 and was scrapped five months later.) You wonder why Nos 1 and 3 Groups persisted with those 'gas' discs? *G. Mastin*

(14) BX KB766 'NA:O' from No 428 ('Ghost') Squadron RCAF, Middleton St George, which met her end when American skipper Flg Off Bob La Turner rode her in at Beauvais Tille having encountered icing en route to Hagen, 2-3 December 1944. *450th Bomb Squadron USAAF via T. J. Allen*

But enough of this preamble. You're not too interested that when production ceased in February 1946 the staggering total of 7,377 Lancasters had been delivered. You *are* concerned that 3,349 failed to return from operations (not to mention innumerable crashes in the UK for one reason or another) . . . that some 15,000 or so lads met their end flying in Lancs . . . that this represents around one quarter of Bomber Command's total dead.

14

16

15, 16 Hercules All Four. Few of you there may be, yet you who knew Hercules rather than Merlins on your Lancs are already feeling left out in this opus! So what that she was an after-thought and totalled a mere 300 in number . . . at 4% little more than a hiccup in total Lancaster production. She had her good points and you swore by her. So you had the usual problems of coring with her radials . . . and used rather a lot of juice; but my, how she climbed . . . and made the 88s and 110s work for their supper before their superior firepower sometimes overwhelmed you. To this day you wonder why their Lordships persisted with .303in pea-shooters when Jerry could stand off at 1,000 yards and knock chunks off you. Whenever you 6 Group types made it to the watering holes of York you were prepared for all the Hally boys' abuse. All in fun, of course . . . and didn't some of your find yourselves converting to Hally IIIs anyway! That wiped the smile off you face for a while . . . but didn't you soon warm to *her*, too . . . once you realised that stabilised yaws — basically bad flying — were a thing of the past now they'd fitted those enormous slab-sided fins and rudders. After all, hadn't you more than once considered the Lanc's tail unit to be her own weakness? If you were in 3 Group and met up with the Merlin Lanc boys from 90 or 218, you countered jibes that your radials glowed at night like rings on a gas stove by pointing out the disadvantages of glycol leaks when a long way from home. You probably covered other topics — like ceiling and all-up weight — but you can't remember . . . and it doesn't matter now anyway.

The business end of 3 and 6 Group Lanc IIs specially for you who knew Hercs. (15) No 514 Squadron's LL678 'A2:L' running up her inners at Waterbeach and soon to perish on Gelsenkirchen, 12-13 June 1944 with Plt Off H. S. Delacour RAAF and crew. (16) DS689 'OW:S' of No 426 ('Thunderbird') Squadron RCAF at Linton-on-Ouse, also to meet an early demise when Flt Sgt M. B. Summers RCAF and crew took her to Stuttgart, 7-8 October 1943, on a one-way ticket. Gauge the sheer bulk of those Hercules 'power eggs', the enormous exhaust stacks, air intakes and oil coolers. Just discernible on DS689 is her bulged bomb bay, fitted to most production BIIs for the carrying of 8,000lb bombs and totally different in shape to those found on Merlin Lancs. LL678, you will observe, has standard profile bomb bay doors.
A. D. Douglas; The Aeroplane

17 You Build 'em . . . We Fly 'em. You expected His Majesty and Winston Churchill to do it; but it came as some surprise when *you* were asked to follow in their footsteps! At any time during your tour, or after, you might find yourselves 'drawing the short straw' (as you thought) becoming the centre of a high-powered official party heading for the factories which turned out the Lancasters you flew. Your brief was simple: go talk to the people whose industry and craftsmanship gave you the tools to do your job of war. Address an assembly of factory workers — thousands of 'em? The mere thought filled you with a dread far worse than ops . . . though you felt easier when you learnt that your whole crew would be in tow, each to say his piece, air his impressions and experiences. A visit from you boys who flew the aeroplanes they built was, you were told, of inestimable value . . . and once there and among all those girls you soon overcame your attack of the jeebies and settled down to enjoy your day. You can believe it, too, when you read that the fair sex accounted for 44% of the work force. You talked to managers and storemen, assembly line workers and capstan lathe operators . . . anyone and everyone . . . all as eager to learn from you as you were to discuss a point or two with them. And there was always the bonus of meeting the man himself — Roy Chadwick, the Lanc's designer — were you to tour AVRO's main factories at Woodford and Chadderton.

Is there anyone who can show you a picture taken that day? Must an oblique of Woodford's apron early in May 1944 be your one reminder? (Second in line nearest camera is BI ME 799, built by Metropolitan-Vickers and assembled at Woodford. She went to No 103 Squadron mid-May 1944 but had met her end before July was out, going down on a Stuttgart raid 28-29 July 1944.)
R. *Boyce*

17

18, 19 Soon for Operations. Experienced as you became at your job — fitter or rigger or electrician, whatever your trade — you were forever learning. Did it seem at times that virtually no two machines which reached you from the six companies turning out Lancasters were exactly alike? As quickly as you genned up on one mod, so there were others to absorb and master. You lost count of the courses you attended at trade-training schools or at A. V. Roe itself. Other mods you learned about when Group sent down one of its technical bods, or you simply worked your way through amendments to an already bulging AP in your section office. Some you already knew about, of course . . . had been embodying for months. You never did understand why it took so long for mods mooted by your own or other squadrons to be incorporated on the production lines. Inevitably, some factories were ahead of others actioning these mods and it was natural kites coming out of Woodford/Chadderton should have them first. You cite, for example, the installation of larger Perspex nose domes (officially Mod 780 and originally designed for the stabilised automatic bomb sight) on BIIIs from the autumn of 1942 . . . simply because AVRO were producing Lancs with Packard-Merlins at the time! Would it surprise you to learn that around one thousand 'improvements' were originated . . . most of them embodied? Not that you remember all that many!

Long after you handed in your spanner or screwdriver does Mod 538 (to invert flame switch), or Mod 810 (sealing of elevator and aileron hinge pins) mean much to you? Other than knowing your service number (can you ever forget it!), perhaps only that for a fizzer — 252 — means anything to you? You do remember the maintenance units, base servicing flights and other units where you effected these improvements as and when. Look in at Ludford Magna and see 1 Group's No 14 Base Servicing Flight at work and renew your hours of slog . . . and comradeship as close-knit as any aircrew. (18) A general panorama, interesting by reason of the two Lancs in the foreground. Nearest is what appears to be BI ME434, which records show to have served only with No 15 Squadron in 3 Group . . . briefly, too, for she did not return from Wanne Eickel, 7 February 1945 . . . little more than one month after being taken

on charge. Directly behind her is a rare BI (BVII interim) from Austin Motors and clearly showing her repositioned dorsal turret. (19) Fully modded Lanc, such as you knew late in the war, about to be aired before delivery to a squadron. Witness her AGLT/'Village Inn' radar below Rose rear turret, IFF 'Z' equipment on nose blister and fuselage-mounted BABS/Eureka homing aerials. Flame dampers have yet to be fitted over each row of Merlin exhaust stubs. *Both E. D. Evans*

21

20-26 Shapes of Things to Come. Remember the excitement on days at advanced flying unit or gunnery school when a Lancaster, Halifax or Stirling lobbed in at your 'drome? You welcomed a break from training to inspect at close quarters the type you would most likely be taking to war sometime in the months to come . . . would come to know more intimately than any Tiger or Oxbox, Gee set or turret you daily did battle with, and at times felt you would never quite master. How close you got to that Lancaster or Halifax or Stirling depended on where she was based, what job she was doing. If she came from a front line squadron, you stood every chance of meeting her crew and persuading them to show you her innards, latching on to their every word, regarding them with awe. However, you needed all your guile to even get close were she from top secret establishments like Boscombe Down or Farnborough. Even if this was not immediately apparent from her exterior, you soon knew something was different when a pair of MPs moved in to stand guard, to keep away the curious. Sometimes it was obvious to the eye she was a 'special' when you noticed 'lumps and bumps' — odd-looking aerials, too, sprouting from fuselage or wings. An age later, when on your tour, maybe your crew found itself dropping in at Boscombe Down or Farnborough when inclement weather closed down your own 'drome and all those around you. Then, with a desire for sleep, the need for food preoccupying your mind, you gave little thought to the weird assortment of kites parked around the field. . . and the last thing you want to see now is a book full of test and development Lancs! But without them you would never have enjoyed the likes of H_2S or Monica, nitrogen tanks or paddle blade props . . . so they played their part just as much as the Lancs which carried you to war.

Here are a few of the specials which helped in developing the Lancaster, or, by the installation therein of apparatus and devices

aplenty, furthered the war effort. (20) BI R5609 which, complete with an aerial array more familiar on Coastal Wimpeys and Liberators, in addition to non-standard bulged bomb bay, made some of you curious during the summer of 1942. Deployed for trials with the Telecommunications Flying Unit before passing to the Aircraft and Armament Experimental Establishment at Boscombe Down on capital ship bombing trials, she reverted to standard with No 97 (Straits Settlements) Squadron (her original unit) until grounded at Blyton as 5288M. *A&AEE*

(21) Another oddity was BIII ED371/G which some of you may have met up with at the Royal Aircraft Establishment, Farnborough a year later. Recognise that nose? Though a mock-up, it was a serious attempt to improve the bomb aimer's visibility (and house a radar scanner), and was to appear on the 'stretched' Lancaster IV, renamed Lincoln, which was too late to see action (with Tiger Force) in the Pacific theatre. Believe it or not, ED371 actually went a few knots faster with such an ugly nose! She, too, would revert to standard configuration and would serve with Nos 207 and 57 Squadrons before being scrapped in September 1946. Not *every* prototype had a yellow 'P' in a circle applied to fuselage sides; nor did every test aircraft with secret equipment aboard carry the suffix 'G' to its serial number as was officially ordered so to be. *RAE*

(22) Unlike the majority of specials, BI W4963 got around a bit. If it wasn't Boscombe Down where you met up with her, maybe it was Canada or the Middle East . . . or was it Hullavington (No 10 MU) where she ended up for scrapping in July 1945, a little over three years after she left Woodford to become a maid of all work with the A&AEE fleet? As for what she did during those three years . . . it's almost a case of 'you name it, W4963 tested it!'. Suffice to say she acted as a 'type trial research vehicle' for the boffins . . . and one day you'll learn why some wag painted 'Bentall's Folly' on her nose, starboard side. *A&AEE*

(23) BI HK543 was another A&AEE workhorse you may have encountered during one of your stooges. At one time or another she must have tested every type of bomb the designers dreamt up . . . including the remotely controlled Azon developed by the Americans and actually used operationally by B-24s of the 8th USAAF. Here, a 12,000lb high capacity bomb drops away from HK543, soon to leave its mark on Ashley Walk range. As with so many of the other specials, HK543 would end her days of usefulness at No 10 MU, Hullavington (December 1946).
Charles Brown

24

(24) Does this Lancaster look familiar? Is she the one you attempted to formate on one day . . . only to stare at in disbelief when she sheered off and revealed four dead props and no visible means of support! If she was painted with a yellow underbelly, wings and tail, you espied BT308/G, the original prototype Lancaster of 1941, enjoying a new lease of life as a test bed for the Metrovick jet engine. See her as she was at the Royal Aircraft Establishment, Farnborough, March 1944 . . . and voice your surprise that no thought was given for her preservation. Ironically, the other wartime jet-powered Lancaster (BII LL735/G, also with a Metrovick mounted in her empennage) continued flying for several years after the war. *RAE*

Finally, to remind you of the enormous contribution made by Rolls-Royce to the Lancaster's success, here are two of many machines which took part in Merlin development and investigation programmes. (25) W4114, originally a BI with Merlin 22s and re-engined in August 1942 to become the official Packard-Merlin

Lancaster prototype and take over from R5849 converted earlier by Rolls-Royce and progenitor of 3,039 BIIIs ultimately produced. The presence of a ventral turret on W4114 tells you she was engaged on turret trials as well as general performance and fuel system analysis when an official photographer recorded her for posterity at Boscombe Down in November 1942. In the hands of aspiring crews passing through Wigsley and Swinderby Con Units, W4114 saw the war out. *A&AEE*

(26) Lancasters on loan to Rolls-Royce could be new machines straight off the production line, or veterans sent to Hucknall as and when the need arose. This is BI ME756 'QQ:B' from No 1651 HCU, Woolfox Lodge, detached to Hucknall January/February 1945. Like the majority of Con Unit machines, she is a cast-off from an operational squadron (in this case No 115, Witchford), and would continue her training role until issued to No 279 Squadron working up on Lancs in Coastal Command, before being sold for scrap in May 1947. *Rolls-Royce*

25

26

Aptitude and Attitude

27 Why are we Waiting. . . ? As firm a devotee as you are, you are well aware that the aircraft you flew, or whose operations you supported, receives far too much attention 40 years on. Like the Spitfire and to a lesser degree the Mosquito, the Lancaster acts as a magnet to authors of novels, television plays . . . even producers of comic strips and jig-saw puzzles for youngsters. Scarcely a week goes by without you reading in your newspaper of a crew being reunited after goodness knows how many years, or some Lanc 'type' getting a mention for whatever reason . . . and you feel not a little guilty! You *know* she was the best . . . yet were not all aircrew the same whichever type they flew into battle? Was not a bowser driver, or the WAAFs who packed your parachute of equal calibre wherever they served? The answer must be 'yes' . . . yet few can deny, there was something about being on a Lanc squadron which gave you an edge, an added confidence. You leave it for others to decide. When thinking back, you realise that chance alone decreed your posting from radio or gunnery school, wherever your training

had been, sent you to an OTU turning out crews for a particular Command and theatre of war. There was no magic formula . . . no earthly reason why a shuffling of the pack should not have sent you to a Hallybag outfit . . . Kipper Kites in Coastal. . . Daks in Burma. Whatever was your destiny, you met the challenge in full. It was after all a matter of aptitude and of attitude.

Canadian Fred Dashper captures the mood of his course, NCOs all, as they await the next train for Swinderby, summer of 1942, there to convert to Manchesters and Lancasters with Nos 61 and 207 Con Flights. Fred and his crew would survive their tour with No 61 Squadron . . . but what of the others here? Does anyone recognise a face? Putting a name to the station is much easier, despite removal of its nameboard — a precaution against enemy agents and reputedly to baffle invaders! It is in fact Lower Heyford, familiar to all who passed through No 16 OTU at nearby Upper Heyford. *F. B. Dashper*

27

28 Big Ain't it! The magic moment has arrived. An aspiring
bomber pilot, you stop to ponder before realising a dream born
some two years ago, when starting out on flying training. All the
sweat and toil, frustrations and setbacks are behind you now as you
set out on the final stage of training. You are about to fly a
Lancaster — an experience never to be forgotten, and almost
equalling the sensation of your first solo at EFTS. First impressions
of the Lanc will be her sheer size, seeming so much bigger than the
Wimpey you have been flying at OTU for the past three months —
a gentle, kindly old kite with only two engines and four other
crewmates to look after. Now you have to cope with four mighty
engines and will be responsible for six other lives. Your excitement
is tinged with just a little uncertainty and apprehension. Even with
300 or so flying hours in your log book now, and considering
yourself a bit of an 'ace' at getting an 'above average' rating at
OTU, it seems, suddenly, there is still a lot to learn, both of the
machine and the men you will be hoping to bring safely through a
tour of ops against colossal odds. This is the final step to the
threshold of flying on ops. What lies beyond: six men looking to
you as captain of a Lanc. How will you respond? Another month
and you will know. One thing is certain: you could not have a better
machine in which to go to war; so it's up to you now. My word, she
looks smooth standing there: yet black and sinister. You've got to
get to know her every quirk and characteristic. She has the
reputation of being kind to sprog pilots, but treat her with respect,
they tell you. Ah yes — there are the ground crew waiting for you,
trying hard to be tolerant with yet another new pilot, but with
obvious misgivings. Well, here goes . . . . *IWM*

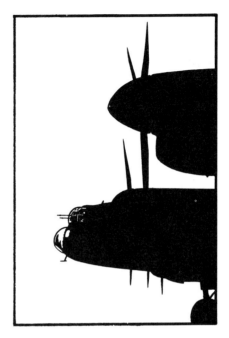

28

29, 30 Almost a Desk Job. Remember how you could barely move or act without there being a form to fill in . . . a chit to sign! Did it appear at times that fighting the war came second to signing for a spanner from the stores . . . that you really hadn't flogged the wrist watch your nav' leader seemed hesitant to write off as unavoidably unaccounted for in a crash you barely escaped from with your life? Did it seem that everything you came into contact with was 'issued for the use of' only when you signed the appropriate form or chit? Nothing and no-one escaped . . . least of all you aircrew. As if you hadn't enough to do, you had even to enter your every flight in a stiff-backed log book. A real bind it was, too, but you're grateful for that record now . . . even if you wonder what you bombed at Villeneuve St George or Flers or Hohenbudberg . . . wherever they were! To fill in your log book, all those forms, in your room, your section was one thing; but didn't your navigator, your flight engineer, too, have to make out their charts while you actually flew on ops! You can see them now: your navigator hunched over his charts and maps, shut off from all that was happening outside his curtained-off compartment . . . appearing no different to WO Kazik Dobrochlop of No 300 (Masovian') Squadron, here (29) preparing for a trip in Faldingworth's briefing room (how many of you kept your Dalton computer?); your engineer, ever solid, ever dependable, recording without fuss his fuel states and temperatures . . . just like No 15 Squadron's Sgt George Pitkin, (30) aboard BI NF953 'LS:A' during a daylight to Wanne Eickel, 7 February 1945. How many of you engineers and navigators thought to ask for your charts when your tour was over . . . wish you had them now, oil, even blood-stained though they might be? For that matter, how many of you air gunners would welcome a look-see at one of your combat reports? Some of you must? *K. Dobrochlop; D. A. Russell*

31 Aloft for the Sheer Joy of Flying. It is probably true to say that you of Bomber Command slot into two distinct categories. There are those of you to whom the war was but a passing phase, an interruption in your life you consider as insignificant as any single seed plucked from a field of corn. For you, eminent surgeon or bricklayer alike, there is no wish for indulgence, no room for sentiment. Those years — your one and only youth — you have shut out of your life as if they never happened. Some of you are bitter; some of you feel cheated. Some of you lead lives of action, fulfilment; some of you lead lives of dread. Whatever your destiny, you have earned your right to peace. Then there are you who regard your part in the air war as the highlight of your life. At no other time, before or since, have you encountered a bond of fellowship, a purpose, a pride, then expected and given without question. You like to believe that never again can you see harnessed such faculties for learning, such mental and moral temperaments combined. Most of you with wings looked on your flying as high adventure; you revelled at the opportunity of emulating the birds — at His Majesty's expense, too! — and you kept your fear of dying in check. Away from the nights of torment, nights when your nerves were more stretched, more taut than the strings of any violin, you soaked up the intoxicating joy of flying in a Lancaster. There was no greater thrill than hedge-hopping virtually at will over farm and fen, enjoying the sight of land girls scurrying for cover from haystacks as you swept by. How tolerant those country folk were!

Before you is 'GI:R', a G-H leader from No 622 Squadron, Mildenhall, winging over the flatlands of East Anglia, autumn 1944. *E. S. Williams*

32, 33 **'Cookie' and Cans.** Preparing your kites for operations did not always go as smoothly as apparent here at Binbrook in 1943, home for the Aussies of No 460 Squadron. Remember the days when nothing went right? What would begin as a routine day could quickly become one of frustration and trouble at every turn, a day when the gremlins were particularly mischievous and continually at your elbow. Whilst you could accept the odd challenge to tax your tired and aching brain early in the morning, you dreaded the day when you might spend hours on your knees or back, contorted in unnatural postures, progressively becoming more irritable as you battled to trace a mysterious electrical fault; or you might have a case of an engine unaccountably surging at altitude, yet which could not be repeated when you went up with the aircrew on test. When these snags occurred you kept going, determined to overcome them, spurred on by the thought of the date you had in town that night. . . . *Both: E. D. Evans*

34, 35   Home was Your Igloo. After the harshness and bull of training camp you could not at first adjust to the apparent laxness of squadron life. Months of square-bashing and kit inspections, assault courses and PT had tuned your mind and body to such peaks of self reliance and discipline your family barely knew you. You were fit, ready to tackle anything, but had yet to adapt to the rigours and routine of an operational station; had yet to make a direct contribution to the war effort. You were soon to find that so long as you did your job no-one bothered you; and you responded with purpose and pride to a freedom without parallel. Not that the interior of your 'igloo' always gave this impression! Be it the Nissen which served as your official sleeping abode, or the shack you erected at dispersal, you were left to your own devices. Such inspections as there were you found to be largely superficial, though when word did go round of a 'big one' you had a scramble to muster the gear! On nights when you could not face the freezing winds or rain, whatever was nature's mood . . . or, when your meagre pay had run out . . . you let go.

(34) A Binbrook or Ludford Magna interior looking rather a shambles but which would be left immaculate when everyone left next morning for the day's work. Here, amid a confusion of drying blankets and wall-slung greatcoats we see two sergeants writing home, another browsing through snapshots, with, beyond, three other NCOs grouped round the ubiquitous coke stove sharing a yarn. *E. D. Evans*

(35) Almost defying description, and far from pleasing to the eye, is a dispersal 'lash-up' at Gransden Lodge as erected by erks of No 405 ('Vancouver') Squadron RCAF who serviced the 'E-Easy' pictured on page 99. Decidedly not a structure such as you were taught to erect when in the boy scouts, yet effective and snug none the less. *S. D. Smith*

36-38 Temporary Reprieve. It did not take you long to learn that to keep your squadron's Lancs flying you had frequently to improvise, be adaptable. When first you arrived at your station fresh out of schools like Cosford, Kirkham and Locking, your head was still full of procedures and practices 'per the book'. You had, perhaps, enjoyed re-rigging the tailplane of a Hart or Audax, or re-wiring a Whitley's electrical system in the relative comfort of an S of TT's workshop. Whether the intention was to mould you into rigger or electrician, engine fitter or instrument wallah, your instruction tended to assume you would always have time on your side, access to unlimited tools and facilities; and, of course, it all looked so easy when demonstrated by an 'old sweat'.

How different it turned out to be when, soon after your posting came through, you found yourself faced with your first problem . . . decidedly uncertain of your ability to cope . . . wondering how on earth the battle-scarred Lanc before you could be back in her dispersal and available for ops when 'Sarge' or 'Flight' said she must. Somehow you did it, thanks largely to your mates, veterans all, but once sprogs just like you. You learned quickly and in no time you, too, were discarding much of your text book learning and adapting to the rigours and vicissitudes of war as it really was. As often as not you would find yourself helping others (remember the call '2-6'?) when a real 'surgery' job came into the hangar.

If you were at Elsham Wolds you may, for instance, recall the hours of toil which went into creating two 'hybrid' Lancs. At least, it seems that two kites were involved but very little positive gen is available as to 'what was fitted to which'! Did BI PD281 'PM:B' really run into BI PD272 'PM:K' during taxying? Was the rear end of PD281 fitted to PD272, or is there in fact a third Lanc involved? Can anyone in our pictures reveal the story? Certainly PD272 was CAT AC 28 October 1944 and left No 103 Squadron's ranks until she returned on 9 December — only to go missing 1 March 1945 during a daylight to Mannheim. PD281 was apparently declared CAT AC 29 November 1944 and was not taken on 103's strength again until 23 December. CAT AC again 28 January 1945, she was sent to A. V. Roe 35 days later. Thereafter PD281 became a nomad, languishing at two MUs before flying to the Middle East (No 135MU, Gebel Hamzi) and ultimate obscurity as 5001M. Sort that out if you can!

Hangar shots at Elsham show: (36) 'new' tail end of PD281 being 'married' to 'PM:B'; and (37) battered rear of PD272 'PM:K' neatly severed at transport joint and suitably propped up. The dog is 'Pickwick', well known to all at Elsham.
R. Brickell via E. Harlin

(38) Finally we have PD281, now 'PM:S', taxying out at Elsham Wolds for a raid during the closing months of the war in Europe, bearing no outward sign of her apparent surgery. *P. P. Hague*

39-40 Path Finder Extraordinaire. While doing your tour you gave little thought to the boys out East fighting the yellow peril. You had your hands full staying alive, living from day to day and could not concern yourself with the poor souls fighting the leeches as well as the Japs. It could so easily have been you out there. They, like you, had no option but to accept where the faceless posting clerks tucked away in some obscure corner decreed you should go. Wherever you went you faced the same fate: death was final. It was the luck of the draw. You found your fellow Aussies and Kiwis who fought their war in the steaming jungles and coral atolls, knowing little of your lot and what you had endured. They were the ones directly protecting your homeland, they considered, while you swanned around Europe, a million miles away, it seemed to them. On returning home for leave after an absence of two years or more, and a hard tour of ops, you found the occasional thread of resentment, even anger running through their number over the apparent indifference to their war shown by authority and the media in Europe. A feeling of wrath even revealed itself on the streets of Sydney or any city or town 'down under'. You could be in

civvies, enjoying a spot of well-earned leave following your tour on Lancs when an irate citizen would toss you a white feather! That hurt, but you held your tongue . . . drawing comfort from the many who shook your hand warmly and acted generously when Lancasters like BIII ED930 (A66-1) and BI W4783 (A66-2) did their bond tours. So, too, did the soon-to-be-famous *Aries* (BI PD328) meet with approval when she circumnavigated the globe during October/November 1944. Few of you serving out your time in places like Honolulu, New Guinea or Samoa — your Lancaster days long over — will forget hearing those distinctive, crackling Merlins once more. Little did you realise you were witnessing the positive beginnings of Tiger Force!

These photographs show *Aries* tethered at Higgins' Strip, Northern Queensland, November 1944, just one of many stop-overs during her fact-finding mission. 'M3' on her nose indicates coding within the Empire Air Navigation School, Shawbury fleet of aircraft types, and soon to disappear when she emerged minus paint and turrets prior to the Polar flights which would make her headline news. *Both: W. L. Hull via F. F. Smith*

42

43

41-43 Lancs for the Memory. Whenever you read of museums appealing for monetary support to help keep them going, do you not find it ironic? It seems incredible, too, that you should be asked to rummage in your attic and hand over that compass or Irvin jacket you feel sure you still have but which you have not even looked at for many a long year. It is not that you begrudge them your money or your relics. You don't. What you do find difficult to accept is that so little remains of the hardware you flew or supported all those years ago. Why is it that so little thought was given to preserving as much a part of your heritage as any campaign of the distant past . . . until it was almost too late! Where are the Whitleys and Hampdens and Stirlings? Why was it the sole remaining Halifax had to be salvaged from a lake in Norway? How different it was in the months after VE-Day. The tumult which followed victory had barely died down when some of you began flying your Lancs to huge graveyards set up at Kemble and other MUs you hitherto never knew existed. Overnight, those self-same workhorses you flew into battle . . . redundant . . . reduced to scrap metal by those of you ending your last days of service there. No praise is enough for a dedicated band of officials and enthusiasts whose foresight and tenactiy of purpose has ensured that generations to come can at least see what a Lancaster and others of her kind looked like.

(41) A once proud lady in the process of being dismantled at Swinderby, autumn 1945. *B. Haslam*

(42) At No 39 MU, Colerne, a good year since he last saw her, flight engineer Graham Robert takes time out to snap the very Lanc he once nurtured on operational duty with No 115 Squadron and which now awaits the axe. *G. Robert*

(43) Finally, we have one which escaped the breakers: B1 R5868 'PO:S' undergoing extensive re-wiring, re-riveting and other essentials by A. V. Roe (probably at Bracebridge Heath) before resuming operational flying with No 467 Squadron RAAF from Waddington, December 1944. Who then could know she would one day dominate the Bomber Hall at The Royal Air Force Museum, Hendon, as a worthy champion of freedom. *J. H. Cox*

44 For the Record. If, for you aircrew there is an abundance of nostalgia or sadness, even bitterness or remorse each time you recall your war with wings, how do you suppose those who assisted and supported you, react when reminded of the part they played? Does a stores wallah or MT driver, sick-quarters nurse or mess waitress even want to remember? Forgotten as they have been for too many years, do they now bother to tell anyone they, too, were there? Is it really as it appears . . . that it is only the fitters and riggers and armourers who tended your kite who turn up at reunions, or make the odd pilgrimage to your old haunts? Do you wonder what became of your adjutant, your barber, your cooks, your clerks? Do they feel as you feel when confronted with a torment of crumbling concrete . . . of rusting corrugated sheeting . . . of total dissolution? Have they stood as you have stood . . . and thought . . . and heard . . . remembered? Have they seen, as you have seen a Lancaster lowering her wheels to land in silence, etched black against a backcloth of sunset when huge spears of light fan down and saturate your mind, your whole being with burning sunlight? Have they wandered as you have wandered over acres of emptiness on days when howling winds failed to drown the murmur of voices coming from your billet, your mess, your section? What does it take to stir a radar mech or instument

fitter? . . . Watching Sgt Aubrey Unwin and LAC Mick Kelly at work on an F24 in Ludford's Camera Section? Perhaps? *V. Redfern*

44

45

46

45, 46 WAAF is as WAAF Does. Why do you suppose no instrument basher, no rigger has written his account of what life was like on a Lancaster station? As much as you regard it important for aircrew to record their memoirs, you consider it high time some of you who stayed with your feet firmly on the ground balanced things up. And what of the WAAFs? Why have so few put pen to paper and renewed your acquaintance with the vital role the lasses in blue performed? Without them cleaning and testing spark plugs, packing parachutes, driving crew buses — the range is endless — no crew, no Lancaster would ever have taken off. You suppose their silence is allied to your own. They, like you are convinced the world of today cares little for what went on in the 'engine room'. Even so, is there no WAAF who can unearth her long hidden diary and tell us what she did, how she lived? Is there no WAAF, keen of mind, keen of effort who, even without recourse to the jottings of youth, feels able and willing to release a tide of memories which will surely follow? You live in hope. Must you all remain unnamed prisoners of history?

Here, but two reminders of the tasks you girls performed so ably. (45) Preparing ration packs for No 101 Squadron crews Berlin-bound from Ludford Magna, 20 January 1944. Who, you ask, is the WAAF? Can anyone name the clerk she is assisting? You wonder how they have fared these 40 years? (46) Still from an official film affording a candid glimpse of Scampton Flying Control some time in 1942. Seated before a cumbersome yet adequate wireless (the word radio came into use later) sits a WAAF operator. Alongside is her time-recording companion and both, you observe, have hair styles far removed from creations so many films of today would have us believe were the standard. Step forward and identify yourselves girls. *R. R. Waughman collection; British Official*

Aids

47 Bowsers, Bombs and Bods. Within months of collecting your demob suit, you marvelled how quickly you had lost your label of 'Brylcream Boys'. No longer were you the local heroes when you went home on leave; no longer were you plied with drinks, allowed entry to cinemas at half price. In quicker time than it took to convert you from raw recruit to tradesman, or see you through training school, you were just one of thousands of redundant servicemen bewildered by an alien world you found it difficult to come to terms with. How different it was when daily the newspapers and newsreels recorded your squadron's exploits, albeit in somewhat pretentious tones. You tolerated correspondents and photographers, journalists en masse, flying with you, following your every move, eager to record on note pad and film all you said, all you did. Ironically, the assemblies of aircraft and equipment you were pictured with serve their purpose from an historical standpoint.

Our study at Scampton in 1945 is typical, though it was mounted for the sole purpose of illustrating a lecture/report by No 1 Group's AOC, AVM R. S. (Bobby) Blucke, titled 'Employment of Strategic

Air Forces in Support of Land Operations'. Flt Lt Les Taylor and some of his No 153 Squadron crew look busy, while the outer petrol tanks of BIII LM550 'P4:C' are filled simultaneously from the 2,500gal AEC bowser. Two engine fitters toil on the port-inner and a third tops up the port-outer's oil tank from the towed bowser visible behind the aircrew. To make ready a complete squadron of Lancs took several hours and it was not unusual for armourers to begin bombing-up while refuelling was still in progress. Thirty-eight years after this picture was taken the hangar and 'married patch' still stand at Scampton; only the trees have changed — now somewhat taller!

The Lanc is of interest on several counts. A veteran of 118 ops, she looks to be in remarkably good shape and is the inevitable mixture of old and new modification standard. Examples externally are the original 'needle' blade props, yet her nose clearly reveals 'Z' equipment, BABS/Eureka aerials, and re-positioned pitot head as being fitted. (LM550 would be scrapped during May 1947.)
F. S. Thornton

48, 49 Distant Relations. How many of you have more than an inkling of all it took to keep your squadron airborne, twice, thrice or more days and nights a week, month after month, year after year? The answer is 'not many'. Come to consider the matter, your own knowledge of the subject is far from exhaustive! In all the months — four, six, nine or more it took to do your mandatory 30 ops (give or take a few), you came to know so very few of those who ran and worked the MT section, bomb dump, tyre bay; even the admin types who paid you and generally pushed around the paperwork, you barely knew — that is unless you had your eye on a WAAF clerk or typist, of course! When you weren't flying you were either preparing for so doing, or training, or sleeping, or in town. How many of you can say you knew well the aircrew whose Lanc stood on the disc of oil-stained concrete next to yours? You shared the same crew bus, swapped the odd laconic quip, and that's about all you knew of them. How few of you knew the lads who manned the aerodrome defence Bofors, ever met those who drove the blood wagons and fire tenders? Not that they expected you to. They were there to support you, knew the pressures you were under. Now, when those of you who attend reunions look out for them, your purpose to buy them an overdue drink, you find them absent. Why, you ask yourself? Where are you boys whose unseen hands flashed your Aldis green, or fired your white scrub rocket and red Very flare with equal skill and care, ensconced within chequerboard-painted caravans like this one at Faldingworth (48), in use by the Poles. Were you at Scampton February 1943, doing your stint with the Chance light, as in this photograph (49)? These and a host of others like them. *Polish Sources; British Official*

48

49

50, 51   Aid and Destroy. The last time you saw displays like these you were fresh out of training school, getting closer to the air war at OTU, or obeying the laws of survival by regularly visiting your safety equipment section on squadron. Such displays you found on every operational station and those acting in a supporting role. There was no easier way for you schoolteachers or salesmen, clerks or shop assistants to make sense of hydraulics and ammeters and circuit-breakers, still something of a foreign language, than studying working layouts like those here in the turret room at No 26 OTU, Wing, May 1944 (actual Frazer-Nash turrets, with attendant hydraulic system and ammo feed, as used on the Lancaster). Until you got to grips with these and like mock-ups you had relied on those of your course who had been tool-setters and planning engineers, men with practical minds and hands, to give you a little coaching in the billet at night. When on your squadron you never forgot your thorough training: as a diligent crew, and as individuals, you continually practised your skills and vital actions until they became automatic. Long hours of dinghy drills and 'action in the event of fire', and familiarity with your safety equipment (as here, displayed for Nos 15 and 622 Squadron crews at Mildenhall, June 1944) just might mean the difference between life and death when trouble came.   *E. G. Dudley; L. E. Chapman*

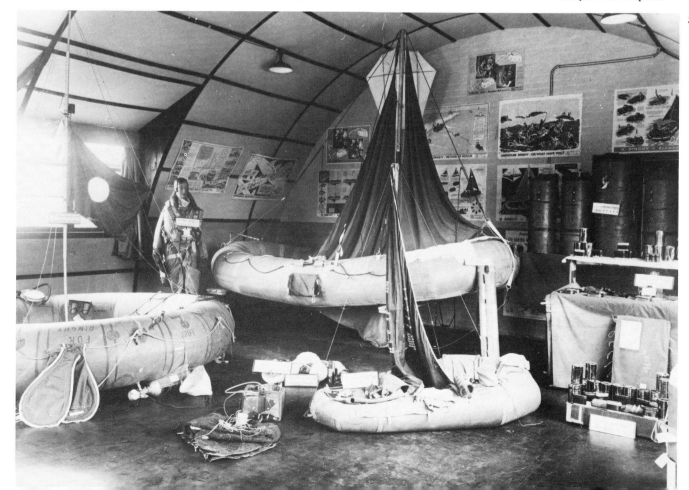

52

52, 53 Ready for Despatch. If it had not sunk in by the time you were posted from Con Unit, you were left in no doubt as to your one purpose in life for as long as it took, as long as you lived, within hours of joining your squadron. From then on, you were told, your sole reason for existing was to unload your bombs on any and every target the powers-that-be directed. Remember your first look at a Lancaster's bomb load? Far from considering what death and destruction that 'Cookie', those cans of incendiaries could do, you wondered only how on earth your Lanc could even take-off carrying such a load. Unless you were around when your OTU got mixed up in the 'one thousand bomber' raids of 1942, and you headed for Cologne, Essen or Bremen in clapped-out Wimpeys or Whitleys, few among you had even seen a live bomb. The only war loads most of you knew were sand-filled 250 and 500-pounders which you dropped by the dozen over ranges whose names you barely remember. There were, of course, the bundles of 'leaflets' you dumped by the hundred over France and Belgium from your Wimpey. 'Nickelling' you called it and perhaps you still wonder what use it was? Even then you were convinced it provided your enemy with you know what! Still, who were you to argue . . . and it did count as your first op! Some of you had seen enough of bombs and incendiaries — ammo, too — even before your tour began. As U/T aircrew waiting for a course, you may have found yourselves joining fellow sufferers humping and stacking — any job which needed doing in bomb dump or armoury. If nothing else you left there with a healthy respect for the lads who never stopped toiling; lads who must have handled so many bombs and incendiaries they dreamt about them, rather than sheep! Did you Lancaster armourers *really* load 51million incendiaries, winch up 608,612 tons of high explosives . . . any numbers of markers and smoke floats . . . as the record books say you did? And, just think, you actually had to sign for every single one (at least your bomb aimer did) before you took off! Though you probably never want to see a bomb or incendiary again, just cast your eye over Kirmington's dump one winter's day in February 1944 and see yourself as an armourer manhandling ice-cold 30lb incendiaries . . . or once more hitch up to a trolley load of 500-pounders as here at Binbrook. . . . *S. S. Bisbee; E. D. Evans*

53

55

54-57 Colours of the Day. If you were operating in daylight in the months following D-Day, the problems of forming up prior to setting course and keeping station within huge gaggles to and from each target soon presented themselves. Experience quickly showed you the need for bright colours, or at least distinctive markings to be applied — just as the Americans had done. You found normal unit codes largely ineffective in other than perfect weather, and then barely visible beyond 500 yards. Naturally you felt reluctant to compromise the dark green/dark earth camouflage and black undersurfaces essential for operating at night. And so the various groups experimented on an individual basis and tried out some bizarre schemes, ranging from smoke canisters in bomb bays were you in the Canadian-manned No 6 Group, to forming up behind a No 635 Squadron Lanc from Downham Market completely decked out in black and white stripes should you be in No 8 Group. No 3 Group specialised in G-H bombing and overcame the problems of identification in two distinctly different ways. With monotonous regularity you flew daylights as vics of three, one G-H Lanc leading two others not so equipped, your leader clearly marked with two yellow bars on her fins. Thus, even if you lost contact with your allotted leader in cloud or through enemy action, you could tag on to another G-H Lanc. Some squadrons experimented with streamers and rockets actually on ops, but it's doubtful if any pictorial evidence is to hand. In Nos 1 and 5 Groups you used tail markings freely, if generally restricted to aircraft flown by senior crews acting as gaggle controllers, and we illustrate a few here to jog your memory.

(54) No 83 Squadron's 'OL:G' from 54 Base, Coningsby, August 1944, sporting white fins and rudders with vertical black bar. Additionally, she has her fuselage identity letter painted white. *A. S. Ridpath*

(55) No 83's sister unit at Coningsby, No 97 (Straits Settlements) Squadron was similarly marked and BIII PB156 'OF:O' is shown in July/August 1944 (Sqn Ldr Harry Locke RAAF and crew), with white fins and rudders and black horizontal bar, white tailplane (with camouflage beginning to show due to engine exhausts), and fuselage identity latter again painted white. (She would survive the war and be sold for scrap at No 20 MU, Aston Down during May 1947.) *T. H. Makepeace*

(56) BIII ND472 'DX:I' from No 57 Squadron, East Kirkby (55 Base), taxying in at Watton on diversion some time in 1944, and complete with dull red fins and rudders and black vertical bar. (She would be destroyed at dispersal 17 April 1945 when PB360 blew up.) *K. Kenyon*

(57) An example from No 1 Group, BIII RE157 'SR:R' of No 101 Squadron, Ludford Magna, circa May 1945. (Scrapped at No 39 MU, Colerne, October 1946.) Colour of this machine's tail uncertain but probably yellow in line with normal 101 practice. The other squadrons making up 14 Base were No 103 using blue, and No 550 using white. All three squadrons extended their use of colours to wingtips and tailplanes. Note how the paint (a form of distemper-cum-whitewash) has been crudely applied, even running on to the fin flash. *C. J. W. Barton*

58

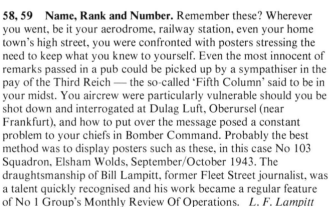

58, 59   Name, Rank and Number. Remember these? Wherever you went, be it your aerodrome, railway station, even your home town's high street, you were confronted with posters stressing the need to keep what you knew to yourself. Even the most innocent of remarks passed in a pub could be picked up by a sympathiser in the pay of the Third Reich — the so-called 'Fifth Column' said to be in your midst. You aircrew were particularly vulnerable should you be shot down and interrogated at Dulag Luft, Oberursel (near Frankfurt), and how to put over the message posed a constant problem to your chiefs in Bomber Command. Probably the best method was to display posters such as these, in this case No 103 Squadron, Elsham Wolds, September/October 1943. The draughtsmanship of Bill Lampitt, former Fleet Street journalist, was a talent quickly recognised and his work became a regular feature of No 1 Group's Monthly Review Of Operations.   *L. F. Lampitt*

59

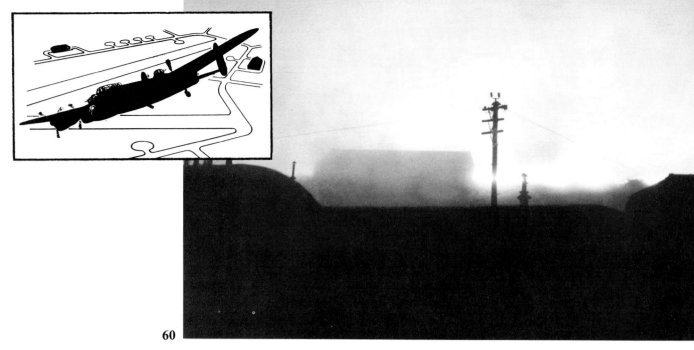

60

60, 61 A Brand from the Burning. FIDO — what memories that conjures up! Born of sheer necessity, FIDO — officially Fog Intensive Dispersal Operation — was one of those inventions (some would say concoction!) which could only become reality during wartime. Brilliant in concept and execution, the enormous monetary costs in petrol consumed (100,000 tons) were far outweighed by the number of crews (actual number not known but 2,486 allied aircraft landed by it), who were able to land on return from operations when their own and most other bases lay beneath a blanket of fog. To land by FIDO for the first time could be quite a hairy experience. Those who had done so before you warned of the treacherous downdraughts caused by the terrific heat generated, swallowing up vital oxygen and rising to uncertain height. It had the effect of pulling your kite down like some enormous unseen hand, making for a bumpy ride and prone to thrust you violently to either side of the pipes if you eased up on your concentration and effort. It was an experience which made you sweat a lot and your eyes, aching from an already tiring trip to the Fatherland, would stand out like organ stops. The heat was intense and could be clearly felt within your Lancaster but the relief once you were safely down was indescribable.

(60) FIDO in operation at 14 Base, Ludford Magna, as viewed at ground level from behind the Camera Section — dramatic even in black and white. You never did understand how fearsome tongues of flame could belch forth from such frail-looking pipe-racks.
V. Redfern

(61) This is Fiskerton, summer of 1944, and the Lancs are from No 49 Squadron . . . but it could just as easily be Graveley and 35, Metheringham and 106 . . . not forgetting the havens at Carnaby, Woodbridge and Manston. *R. A. Denny*

61

Nationalities

62 Timely Punch. When nightly you sat before your TV screens watching the recent Falklands war 'as it happened', were you not amazed — sometimes horrified — how every decision, every action came under scrutiny by probing cameras and commentators as well as being debated by experts and laymen alike? You leave it for others to decide the merits of such freedom, but did it not roll back the years to the time *you* were at war?

Think about it . . . in some ways you came out of it knowing little more than the day you enlisted! Generally you knew only your squadron and it took you a decade, probably more, to learn some of the 'facts and figures'. Perhaps it's as well you knew so little . . . judging by all you since learn from the writings of your champions, your critics. Yet still there remain questions — minor and major — unaswered. Take, for example, the Lancaster's very introduction to squadron service. A daring daylight to Augsburg on 17 April 1942 by Nos 44 and 97 Squadrons you read about in the newspapers (suitably censored), of course. But has anyone, any source told you why 44 was selected to pioneer the Lanc in squadron service? A minor question? . . . perhaps? Does it matter? . . . maybe not! Yet you would still like an answer, and you wonder if it lies in once-secret files now open for inspection.

That 44, with a growing affiliation to Rhodesia and its sons, should be selected, was a popular move you have little doubt. How long did it take you, however, to learn that the honour of leading them into battle fell to an Englishman: Wg Cdr R. A. B. Learoyd? With the highly prized ribbon of the Victoria Cross on his chest, 'Babe' Learoyd was evidently an ideal man for the job and he gathered around him men of equally wide experience. Almost all had a tour of ops (in the main Hampdens) behind them, a mixed bunch of prewar regulars and early volunteers, Britishers and Rhodesians alike. Many had been detached to Boscombe Down during trials there with the two prototypes (BT308 and DG595) and converted quickly and efficiently by flying with the A&AEE test pilots; others did their familiarisation at Waddington when BT308 was detached for the purpose and, despite there being no comprehensive pilots' notes (save for the briefest scribbled handling notes) during those early months, few had difficulty graduating from twins to fours, along with adjusting to the added weight and size and complexities.

Thus began the opening rounds of endless circuits and bumps you men were to do in Lancasters . . . as here early in January 1942 with BI L7538 'KM:B' climbing out of Waddington. Number 12 off the production line, and one of the initial three Lancs delivered to No 44 (Rhodesia) Squadron Christmas Eve 1941, she was to be an early casualty when overshooting on 20 February 1942 and declared CAT E. *M. R. James*

63 Mask of Death. From all over the world you came, eager and willing to carry the fight to the common foe. Your backgrounds varied enormously and to list them all would fill a book: engineers and plumbers, schoolteachers and lawyers, coal miners and bricklayers, office clerks and local government officers, volunteers all, who quickly swelled the ranks of a rapidly expanding Bomber Command besides filling the gaps left by the prewar career regulars who had formed the nucleus when the conflict began in September 1939. Large numbers of you were boys straight from school; boys with little experience of life but who matured almost overnight . . . if you survived long enough.

This is Newfoundlander Plt Off Fred Mifflin of No 106 Squadron in joyous mood on return from Magdeburg 21-22 January 1944, masking his tiredness for the benefit of press photographers on hand at Metheringham to observe and record the night's operation. Miff, as he was known, was a typical product of the Empire Air Training Scheme, quietly tough and gutsy, full of life and with so much to give. Even on their first trip, Leverkusen 22-23 August 1943, the Mifflin crew hit trouble, being jumped at extreme range by a fighter whose attack damaged the Lanc's starboard wing. Unhappily, they were doomed, as were so many fine crews of the period, going down on Schweinfurt 26-27 April 1944. It would have been their 25th completed operation. Among the five crew members who survived to become PoWs was flight engineer Sgt Norman Jackson whose heroic action that night later earned him a Victoria Cross; but, sadly, skipper Fred Mifflin and English gunner Flt Sgt 'Johnny' Johnson were not among those to survive. Observe the amusing yet graphic explanatory posters on the wall of the interrogation room in our picture. *E. Sandelands*

64-68 Some of You lived . . . Some of You Died. Be honest: who among you, at some time or other during your long months of training, did not have your say about the mandarins who sat in judgement on you at Air Ministry, Kodak House, and other corridors of power? What had drill on the promenade at Torquay to do with manning a gun turret? Why send you to places like Gunter Field, States-side, where you were made to eat in silence like naughty schoolboys despite being near to becoming fully fledged pilots? Who else could dream up the notion that up to a hundred of you could be shut in a room or hangar at OTU and told to form yourselves into crews? But, incredibly, it worked! Just as you later came to appreciate that much of the bull and restrictions of your early service was essential for developing self reliance and inner discipline, so you gave thanks to the self-same 'shiny arse brigade' whose wisdom led you to your crew. Even before you entered that room, that hangar, you had perhaps sought out the soft spoken Kiwi you had seen sitting it out with a book in the mess, and agreed to team up with . . . or enjoyed playing shove ha'penny in the local pub with a couple of hard drinking Canucks who looked capable if anyone did. However your crew formed, be it one of four, even five Aussies and one Pom, or five Poms and one Aussie, you rarely regretted your choice. No Air Force, before or since, has sent into battle men from a hundred nations . . . volunteers all, whose involvement and call to arms continually baffled your enemy. Were you to enjoy the hospitality of Dulag Luft, you will recall the look of disbelief on the faces of your interrogators when confronted with a ranch-hand from Patagonia, a lawyer from Cape Province! Nor, too, could they understand how or why a student from Oslo should be navigating a Lancaster . . . a storeman from Geelong man a Marconi set.

On this page, just a handful of names and faces to remind you of the finest band of men it has been your privilege to know. Study their faces and see again a certain bomb aimer from the prairies of Manitoba singing his heart out 'three sheets to the wind' in the lounge of the 'Marquis of Granby'; a clown, full of fun, yet who one night came back from Leipzig with flak splinters in both legs and suffered in silence until you were out of harm's way. Or a rough, tough miner from Broken Hill winning a wager by walking the entire length of Huntingdon High Street on his hands (big as clams they were) just one night away from being blown to bits somewhere over the Ruhr. Memories you hold dear whatever the critics of Bomber Command level at the campaign you fought.

(64) Plt Off Esmond Farfan came from Trinidad to fight with Bomber Command and left No 12 Squadron, Wickenby early August 1944 having completed a not uneventful but fairly routine tour for the period. Restless within weeks of beginning his mandatory six-month 'rest' period, and pressing for a second tour, he had barely started flying Mossies with PFF when hostilities ceased. He returned to his native land determined to continue flying and exchanged bombers for airliners, which he flies to this day, as well as help run a well-established family firm. Here he puts in some practice at the shooting butts. Remember those .38 Smith and Wessons you at one time took on ops? *E. K. Farfan*

(65) Delightful study of two No 9 Squadron skippers relaxing outside the Officers' Mess at Bardney, Spring 1943. At left, without battle-dress, is Plt Off Bob Van Note, a Yank from Boulder, Colorado, who volunteered for flying before his own country entered the war. 'Van' would leave Bardney at the end of his tour and transfer to the USAAF — only to die tragically. On his left sits Sqn Ldr Murray Hobbs, an irrepressible New Zealander from Christchurch, who ran 'A' Flight until his Lanc was blown apart on Gelsenkirchen, 25-26 June 1943. *J. H. Moutray*

65

(66) Plt Off F. C. G. DeBrock (known as 'The Count' — perhaps he was?) came from Belgium to fly with the RAF but sadly registered his name among the missing when the Lancaster of which he was engineer went down on Revigny, 14-15 July 1944. He was by then a qualified path finder with No 156 Squadron, Upwood, to whom he was posted following his term as engineer leader with No 101 Squadron, Ludford Magna (where this portrait was posed). *Popperfoto*

(67) Flt Sgt Tapua Heperi, a Maori from The Bay of Islands . . . big of heart, big of stature . . . as good a man as you could have on the Marconi of a Lanc. Fellow Kiwi Flt Lt Dave Clement was his skipper and their crew — three Englishmen and four New Zealanders — left Mepal and No 75 Squadron in one piece. 'Tap' Heperi cut an imposing figure and it did not take long for New Zealand's official war artist Peter McIntyre to seek him out as suitable 'copy'. You wonder if the canvas he painted can be viewed today? Tap was a true gentleman and it will come as no surprise to all who knew him to learn that he took illness and a long spell in hospital soon after returning home completely in his stride. Undaunted, his firm resolve saw him succeed as a farmer, and find time for community work on behalf of his race and the Mormon Church, later recognised by such appointments as Chairman of the Tai Tokerau Maori Council, Mormon Bishop and high councilman. He is gone now . . . sorely missed by his people. Remember him as he was on return from an Essen daylight, 11 March 1945.
D. S. C. Clement

(68) Flt Lt Roy Hare preparing for Berlin in Bottesford's locker room, spring 1943. 'Juggo', from Stourbridge, Worcs and all that epitomised an Englishman, served No 467 Squadron RAAF with distinction during his tenure as gunnery leader, but volunteered for one op too many and died with CO Wg Cdr J. R. Balmer RAAF, attacking Bourg Leopold, 11-12 May 1944. *W. H. Hare*

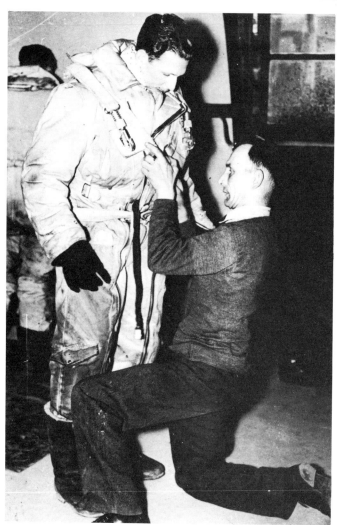

C Conversion

69 ... And Still They Come. Despite the prospect, at best, of an uncertain future, there was never a lack of volunteers to join the ranks of aircrew. It was a strange fascination — almost a compulsion — which drew you young hopefuls of the Commonwealth and beyond. For many, it was the realisation of boyhood dreams after reading the exploits of the men who flew the 'stick and string' biplanes in World War 1. For some of you the dreams began on seeing Sir Alan Cobham's flying circus or attending memorable between-the-wars air displays. However, in the main it was an opportunity for you surveyors or accountants, car mechanics or plumbers, farm-hands or grocer's boys to become a member of a fraternity far removed from your peacetime world — a world you would never have considered leaving — unless you had the necessary qualification, background and aptitude to join the Reserve. There were even some of you who volunteered to fly because the prospect of being holed up in a trench, below decks in a destroyer, even down the mines, was far from attractive!

Here we see Flt Sgt Ray Barlow RNZAF and crew with their allotted aircraft for the day's training flight, at No 1653 HCU North Luffenham, set in the delightful undulating countryside of Rutland, April/May 1945. Mid-upper Sgt Paul Vermuelen takes it easy, almost hidden by swaying uncut grass on the edge of the dispersal, while engineer Ted Cornell chats with the groundcrew. The Barlow crew, posted to No 101 Squadron, Ludford Magna, arrived too late for operations against the enemy; their nearest 'action' was to take part in Operation 'Wastage', the dumping of bombs in Cardigan Bay, etc. Note the rather battered paintwork on the Lanc here pictured. *C. J. W. Barton*

69

70 Fly You Must. It was at places like Sandtoft that you were introduced to your engineer and your team of seven learned to master a Halifax, sometimes a Lancaster, it depended when you were there. Seven men, a team equally as deadly as the dashing fighter pilot you each saw yourself becoming that day you signed on to accept the King's shilling. You left there — you lucky ones who earned yourselves a Sandtoft Survivor's Medal — no longer raw — your keenness blunted . . . yet determined to press on and be damned. As at OTU you flew so much and so hard and in such weather and under such conditions that you climbed out of your aircraft exhausted — even shaking after the immensity of the struggle it had forced you to wage both with it and yourself. You flew when it was so cold your sandwiches froze into inedible chunks of bread and pastry meat and had to be flung out. Take care not to damage the props, they said! You flew when it was so cold you dare not remove a glove for more than a few minutes for fear of frost-

bite. You flew in the mornings, in the afternoons, in the evenings and at nights. And it was at Con Unit you said hello to the old boy with the scythe. A lot of good blokes died at Con Unit. A *lot* of good blokes. One minute a kite would be rounding out for a landing on three engines . . . the next a tangled, tortured pile of melting metal and flame in the mud at the end of the runway, writhing under the water-streams of the defeated fire-hoses. Kites would take-off on a routine training flip. Up to Scotland and back and just under eight hours to do it. But a lot of you didn't. A lot of you met hills in low cloud, and a lot of you ran out of petrol over the sea because someone had boobed. And a lot of you went for the chop just because the aircraft had packed up beneath you . . .

Here taxying past the Sandtoft watch office is No 1667 HCU's 'GG:X' on a day when anyone with any sense (or a good excuse!) is under cover — anywhere but out in the muck and murk.
F. G. Christy

70

71

71 The Black Side. Even before your crew faced the enemy on operations your long training period was fraught with dangers. Not least of these was the ever-present threat of collision in the crowded skies over Britain. The ever changing weather did not help, a continual challenge during the course of a cross-country exercise, a bullseye, or practice bombing stooge to Wainfleet or Misson. Did you not have enough to do coping with the mysteries of Gee, sorting out boosts and revs and a seemingly endless range of tasks and functions — all to be mastered in the process of moulding your crew into an effective fighting unit — without interference from the elements and other bods engaged on their own detail! At the best of times, in open skies, you had to keep a sharp eye out for other aircraft, fast or slow, large or small — balloon barrages too — a discipline which had quickly to become second nature and would certainly save your life on more than one occasion during your tour.

Here is a typical casualty of the period, in this case a Manchester (L7453) from No 1661 HCU, Winthorpe which collided with a Halifax in the circuit on 1 May 1943. Following their withdrawal from operations, Manchesters filled an important role at Con Units, though the type was never totally reliable, even with downrated Vultures and many a crew had a nasty fright during such exercises as a night cross-country or a loaded climb. Note the badly flaked black 'night' finish on L7453; also that the unit code letters (GP) still appear to be painted grey and not dull red as ordered to be applied from spring 1942. *D. Grant*

72 What Lies Beyond? Any picture is worth a thousand words. How often have you heard this said? All you know is that, for you, none can fully recapture the memories — once vivid, now waning — each one of you has of Con Unit. Can any canvas give you a feel for the wearisome hours you spent by day and by night on endless circuits and bumps until you knew every tree, every field as well as you got to know a Halifax or Stirling? Can anyone show you a picture which sends a shiver up your spine as you recall the nightmares of bullseyes executed in the most atrocious weather; the loneliness of night flight, tuning your minds and bodies for all that lay ahead in the months to come. No snapshot can fully convey the bleakness of winter at places like Riccall and Wratting Common, so cold you had first to break ice before you shaved each morning . . . or building up your biceps chopping wood in your desperate efforts to keep the billet stove fed with fuel when coke supplies ran out. So it is when you visualise losing the battle against earwigs, thousands of 'em which plagued you in summer at Balderton and Wigsley.

What do you see when you look at a cockpit vista of Winthorpe such as this? Do your eyes search beyond the Lancs (and some Manchesters barely discernible in the distance) of No 1661 HCU, here silent in windswept bays? A vision, perhaps, of seven youngsters sealing your bond of fellowship and trust in the 'White Hart' at Newark following your first day airborne as a crew of seven . . . or renewing your first encounter with a Lanc . . . exploring her every inch, her sounds, even her smells . . . remembering now happy — and relieved — you all were to be flying her . . . . *J. R. Gray*

72

73   **War of the Roses.** Infrequently pictured together are the two aircraft which bore the brunt of Bomber Command's offensive from 1943 onwards. For you Lanc men who flew both, opinion on which was the better type is somewhat clouded because of the clapped-out Hallies you struggled with at Con Units (the same can be said of the Stirling). Additionally there were the limitations of the early Merlin Hally IIs and Vs, appearing 'gutless' and prone to disastrous stabilised yaws. In fairness it must be said that few of you had the chance to handle the later Hercules-powered IIIs and beyond — vastly improved machines, full of power and punch. The Halifaxes here featured are BV series II (Special) variants from No 1656 HCU, Lindholme, retrospectively fitted with square fins and rudders to overcome the dreaded rudder locking. The Lancaster is BI ME812 'AS:F' from No 166 Squadron, Kirmington, and the picture was almost certainly taken at Linton-on-Ouse, 20 June 1944, to which airfield Plt Off Sid Coole and crew diverted due to bad weather following an abortive trip to a V1 site. Coole and crew 'used up' two 'Fair Fighter' Lancs during their tour — that pictured here being their second and destined to survive the war as a centenarian. (It was broken up at No 20 MU, Aston Down, October 1946.)   *R. J. Russell*

74   Some You Walk Away From. Were some crews fated?
Certainly for some of your fraternity trouble was never far away.
Right from commencement of initial training you had found that
some chaps seemed accident prone and were forever in difficulties.
If anyone had to get lost because of inclement weather while on a
cross-country, or suffer a ground loop due to a burst tyre, you
knew who it would be. If, when you gathered around the bar in the
evenings, you did not debate the subject, then your instructors
certainly would. Your mentors could generally tell which crews
were going to make it through a tour (discounting luck) and when,
many months later, you, too, found yourself elevated to the grade
of instructor you also could predict with uncanny accuracy the
lifespan of your student crews. Of course, it did not follow that an
accident-prone crew was of poor quality. Take that headed by Plt
Off G. J. Chequer for example. They *were* a good team, yet
appeared decidedly fated. They had survived a wing spar cracking
while on an OTU training flight in a Wellington, in addition to a
near mid-air collision with a Martinet engaged on a drogue-towing
stooge (and resultant entanglement with the cable) even before
converting to Lancs! Posted to No 1678 Heavy Conversion Flight,
then based at Little Snoring, the Chequer crew — now seven in
number with the inclusion of a flight engineer — soon found
themselves *in extremis*. While on a routine exercise, 2 September
1943, flying BII DS608 'O-Oboe', they suffered an engine failure in
flight. By now leading a well disciplined crew, Chequer carefully
positioned his mount for a landing — only to experience loss of all
brake pressure.

The result is pictured. (Interestingly, close inspection of the
picture reveals an unidentified code combination. Evidently
No 1678 Con Flight used other than 'SW'.) Arriving on No 514
Squadron, Waterbeach when the Battle of the Ruhr was giving way
to an even more awesome target, the Chequer crew's luck ran out
on 30-31 January 1944 when they failed to return from Berlin.
K. B. M. Grant

75 Peace and War. Blyton . . . Lindholme . . . Wombleton . . . once, briefly, familiar names, now all but forgotten . . . each with its own poignant memory for you budding aviators experiencing life as a crew of seven for the first time prior to taking on the enemy for real. More often than not it seemed to be the elements you were fighting and it is likely your main memory of HCU is of a two-month period of intensive flying in the most appalling weather. Looking back you well realise that HCU was merely an extension of OTU — even to its ground staff and instructors who seemed always to exude a perpetual air of dejection, longing to return to an operational squadron. The difference was that whereas your OTU had generally been in the delightful Cotswolds or on the East Midland plains, within easy reach of any number of towns and cities, Con Unit seemed invariably to be located at the bleakest, most inaccessible aerodrome it was possible to find. Forty years on you view a scene overpowering both in size and loneliness; a wide, unending plateau which fills you with both pleasure and sadness. Pleasure when you recall that it was here your fledgling crew left the nest of learning and moved on to earn its keep over Germany; sadness as you remember those crews who didn't make it and died hereabouts in kites long past their prime, hand-me-downs just about ready for the scrap heap . . . and you reflect how incongruous it was for Nissens and dispersals to nudge a field of barley or mingle with nature at a woodland's edge — though you feel sure you were too busy, too absorbed with your flying, your few nights in town, altogether too detached from the world outside to realise it at the time.

Try if you can to identify this corner of Sandtoft should you wander from the National Trolley Bus Museum now in residence at the field you called Prangtoft . . . or dip into your memory for the rumble of the Lancs and Hallies of No 1667 HCU you once knew. *Mrs B. Hollows*

76

76 Every One a Greaser. You laugh about it now . . . your first 'conversion' to service life. Remember proving to the medics you had two of everything you should have in that never-to be-forgotten room above Burton's, wherever your medical was conducted! Next came Lord's cricket ground or similar sanctums for ITW. (How can any country lose a war when it ropes-off 22 yards of hallowed turf and you are told it is required after hostilities have ceased!) Thereafter, it was one course, one conversion after another . . . and up to the time you arrived at OTU as five separate brevets barely soiled since awarded your one wing, or two, you had yet to learn your fore-ordained lot. It hadn't even occurred to you that each OTU turned out crews for a particular Group or Command, at home or overseas . . . if indeed you were bothered! You were committed and would fly anything their lordships gave you . . . though some of you perhaps prayed it would be Lancs and not Hallies or Stirlings . . . unless the lure of Coastal Catalinas or Liberators with their ashtrays as well as galleys proved too much for you!

Many of you engineers did, of course, actually have your choice of aircraft when at St Athan . . . that is dependent on which letter of the alphabet your surname began with, or what day of the month your birthday fell on: thereby hangs a tale! Even when you knew you would be flying Lancs on ops, most of you faced a temporary setback when, on arrival at Con Unit, you found Stirlings or Halifaxes, even Manchesters in use. Big and black and wicked they

were, too. Lancs, you found, were still one step, one conversion away. And so, most of you did not step inside Chadwick's wonder until you reported to Lanc Finishing School. You took to her at once and needed little more than a week, 10 days at the most, to understand her, discover her secrets, appreciate her forgiving ways. Not that you had it easy. Above all you had to familiarise yourself with something called idle cut-off action when your kite had Packard-Merlins. It's all rather hazy now but you do recall what happened on take-off when a crew forgot! You could not rely on being allocated a BI with Rolls-Royce-built Merlins, which didn't overheat so readily on your continual circuits and bumps . . . like this, at No 5 L F S, Syerston some time in 1944.

. . . and so to your squadron. *W. G. Gardiner*

Camaraderie

77 Horse Play. Your crew — what vivid memories that must evoke for you ageing veterans who long ago rode the war-torn skies of Europe and experienced a bond of friendship and mutual trust the like of which may never happen again. You were seven men brought together by conflict and you came to know each other's every mood and reaction, ability and humility, likes and dislikes during your training and operational life together; you were seven men who probably knew more about each other than your own mother knew about *you*. When you left home you were but boys, untested in endurance and courage and fear — real, naked fear — and you were 'marked' for the remainder of your natural life... those privileged few of you who survived. Your crew — seven men who not only flew together but ate, drank, slept and played together. You were 'one' and generally inseparable; rank meant little between you, yet you knew the dividing lines between respect, authority and familiarity. At the time it seemed it could never end, and yet, when your tour was over you would say goodbye with a handshake, rarely to meet again.

Here we see some of Flt Lt Eddie Tickler's No 57 Squadron crew enjoying themselves at East Kirkby circa March 1944. For them there would be no handshakes, for their luck ran out on the infamous Nuremberg debacle of 30-31 March 1944, going down to the cannons of a Messerschmitt Bf110 night-fighter. Four men died that night — their 13th of a 30-trip tour — though they were the only crew lost from 57. Within a few days a new Lancaster had replaced BIII ND 622 'DX:E' and 'The Jampot and the 7 Raspberries' (which stemmed from Eddie Tickler being a member of the Tickler Jam Company) became but a memory. *E. W. Tickler*

A Complement of Seven

Space precludes mention of the relatively few eight-man crews who included in their number a special operator to man the 'Airborne Cigar' equipment installed in No 101 Squadron Lancasters; also some experienced PFF Crews who carried a visual bomb aimer on daylight operations.

Pilot: What He Says Goes: What He Does Counts

Who is the man up front, this Driver-Airframe?
Pilot? Captain? What's in a name?
Let's say he's just another member of the crew,
But this description simply will not do.
He's trained to fly this kite — agreed,
But more, much more, he's there to lead;
To bring us back unscathed and sane,
Not once, but time and time again.
We looked to him for miracles of mind and will,
For deeds beyond the range of human skill;
What words of ours describe him well?
No words suffice: we called him 'Skip'
*   and followed him to Hell.*

Philip A. Nicholson

Navigator: To Guide You There and Back

Intent in his lamplit berth
He plies his precise trade
With dogged skill,
His steady nerves and nimble brain
Manipulating the cyphers of his craft.
Blind to the ground he covers,
He brings us unerringly
To an exact rendezvous and home again,
Battling against darkness,
Contrary winds, fatigue, and the
Burden of our total trust.

Philip A. Nicholson

Bomb Aimer: He Who Justifies the Means

His is the act that justifies
The journey:
The skill that deals the hammer blow.
From base to target zone he
Plays small part,
But then, down in his cramped station,
Riveted to his bomb sight, prone,
Vulnerable, oblivious to all, except
the need to run up straight
And hit the mark, the stage is his;
The whole excuse for his existence
Concentrated in the brief pressure
Of an eager thumb.

Philip A. Nicholson

Wireless Operator: A Good Listener and Vital as a Watch

Cocooned in a capsule of noise,
Straining his ears through static
For the frail thread of Morse,
He keeps his solitary listening watch,
Coaxing, with skilful fingers,
Strength into feeble signals.
Humoured as the dot-dash boffin
The eccentric key-basher, the fetch and carry
merchant,
He soldiers on unappreciated, until, one rough trip,
Hit over the target, navigator half-dead,
Kite blown off course and pilot lost,
He brings them home on loop bearings
And fixes, to be known ever after
As, the 'gen man'.

Philip A. Nicholson

Flight Engineer: An Airborne Plumber — No Less

Of all of us, the engineer
Knew most about the aircraft gear;
Dials and switches, props and flaps
The drill if undercarts collapse.
What to do when fuses blow
Or overstressed components go;
Coping when hydraulics fail
Or bits fall off a damaged tail.
Oxygen, electrics, fuel,
Engines running hot or cool;
Something odd about the trim
All these queries came to him.
His duty, too, it was to share
His skipper's vigil in the air;
Providing one more pair of eyes
To scan the dark and dangerous skies.
A man of many parts who knew
His worth to pilot, plane and crew.

Philip A. Nicholson

Air Gunners: Behind the Brownings' Bark

Alone in his transparent shell,
A speck in space,
He sits, poised in his airy kingdom;
At his back the unknown,
Before him the unfolding map
Of his journey.
Guardian of seven lives,
Taut with the concentration of survival,
He swings his turret through vigilant arcs,
Eyes straining for the fighters,
Braced for the violence of surprise.

Philip A. Nicholson

78

79

78, 79 Lazy Bones. That war is 1% action and 99% boredom is an oft-quoted phrase. True or not, there certainly were periods of inactivity during Bomber Command's sustained offensive. You tend to forget countless hours spent lying on your pit when outside the fog was so thick you could barely see your hand in front of your face. It sometimes lasted for days on end and, while operations would be repeatedly put back until finally abandoned for the day, you had still to hang around until the evening when the liberty bus would take you into Lincoln, Nottingham, Cambridge, wherever. You had generally completed your DIs by lunch time and the afternoons tended to drag as you maybe added a lick of paint here, or tidied up there in your section. Equally a bind were lectures on safety equipment, intelligence, or how to act should you end up behind the wire. You regarded these very much a bore but for some of you they would prove invaluable. Then there were the lulls brought about because it was physically impossible to mount operations every single day and night; at other times such enforced spells of quiet might be through awaiting a call from the Army for aerial support as its advance ebbed and flowed. Whatever the reason you read every book and magazine you could get your hands on, played cards or draughts, or simply slept . . . anything to pass the time. Often you thought it would never end.

Illustrated are air and groundcrews inert for totally differing reasons: (78) erks enjoy a brew, probably at 14 Base, Ludford Magna, while (79) No 12 Squadron aircrew 'in limbo' at Wickenby during the same period, late winter 1944/spring 1945.
E. D. Evans; C. E. Jones

80 Lie in the Dark and Listen*. It was comforting to know that the folk who lived on the fringe of your world — a world of noise and anxiety and fear and dread — in villages you knew as well from the air as you did on the ground, could accept you so readily. They, and others equally warm-hearted who farmed the land right to your aerodrome's perimeter, were so tolerant of your wild antics, your boisterous behaviour. Your blue-clad hordes far outnumbered them, dominated their community, seemingly had more freedom of movement; yet, regardless of the hour, they would lie abed counting you in. Hearts would miss a beat on hearing one of *their* crews in trouble, and when the inevitable happened, you could be certain of having one or more of these simple-living people appear first on the scene of your crash. You would not be surprised to find them arrive by tractor or on horse-back, dressed in little more than night attire, proffering what help they could.

Here, a Lanc from Binbrook, wheels and flaps down on final approach, passing low over not so dormant village cottages as the first ribbon of light is visible on the skyline to herald a new day. You remember well bearing witness to the phenomenon of two sunrises. You would already greet the first sunrise when aloft, letting down when still some way from base. Once down and through interrogation and breakfast you would again see the comforting glow appear majestically above the horizon. Another dawn would be breaking as you prepared to enter darkness of a more pleasing kind — the peace and relief of deep sleep.
L. E. Aitken

*With apologies to NC.

81, 82 Lobbing In. Despite the constraints of war you had a quite remarkable freedom of movement and action when on your squadron. Should you be on good terms with your CO or Flight Commander, you could often hitch a ride to an aerodrome near your home in a Lanc whose crew was scheduled for a cross-country or bombing detail. When you look back you marvel at all the wangles which went on, both with and without approval. It was so easy, while on an air test, even a supposed simulated Y-run, to lob in somewhere and visit a pal bored with instructing at OTU, and allow him the feel of a Lanc again. For you who were stationed near the 'Fort' and 'Lib' bases of the 8th US Army Air Force there was, of course, the added attraction of sampling food you saw only in Hollywood movies, or dreamed about. They, in turn, found any excuse to drop in on *you*, eager to swap their Cokes for your 'warm' beer! Next morning promises made around the bar would be

fulfilled and you would inspect and maybe wring out each other's kites before going your separate ways. If your Lanc was a Hercules-engined BII you really did find yourself the centre of attraction. Well acquainted as your American cousins were with Lancasters — stationed at places like Methwold or Little Staughton you were near neighbours — a Lanc with radials was something else, a distinct novelty! Indeed, many of you Merlin-Lanc men never saw one!

Shown are evocative shots of BII DS842 'JI:F', *Fanny Firkin II*, from No 514 Squadron, Waterbeach: (81) ghosting in at Deenethorpe, Northants, 3 May 1944, and (82) being inspected by B-17 men of the 401st Bomb Group. DS842 (regular mount of Plt Off Bob Langley and crew for 18 ops February-June 1944) just failed to see the war out, being struck off charge in March 1945 when with No 1668 HCU. *Both: USAF*

83 Close to Home. If you were lucky your dispersal was close to a farm or outlying cottage. You remember lazy days down at the flights, hanging around while waiting for the groundcrew to complete their DIs, leaving you free to run through your own checks. You maybe passed the time of day with the farm-hand working the field beyond, or shared your chocolate left over from the last trip with children who daily came from the local village to group at the barely adequate fence which separated your two worlds. Mid-morning, losing patience with the tea van taking its time to reach your dispersal, you maybe slipped quietly away along the well-worn path to the farmhouse which had become a second home to you, there to munch on a real pork pie or savour a still warm, freshly baked cake put your way by the farmer's wife who treated you like her own son. You have warm memories of those country people who took you into their hearts and homes and were your link with sanity and peace. You recall with gratitude evenings sitting before an open fire tucking into suppers of ham and pickle and quaffing home-made beer or potato wine . . . and you feel guilty not having kept in touch. When you did attempt to seek them out as men of mature years — very much the age they must have been when you were a callow youth — you were too late; they had left this earth we know. Yet, you feel sure they understood and forgave you.

Featured is No 12 Squadron's 'PH:U' pointing her nose towards a farmstead well known to Wickenby men, and still there today, long after the aerodrome is little more than a landing strip for light aircraft, largely returned to the land.   *G. Mastin*

83

84

85

84, 85   You and Yours. If the likes of rabbits and monkeys — any one of a dozen or more straw-filled mascots — were not in your line, perhaps your crew preferred a real live dog? Offhand you cannot think of a single station on which you served which was not without its collections of dogs and cats, even goats and ducks. It was another precious link with the life you had left behind you, a life you hoped to resume just as soon as you could put this war behind you. Where they came from was often a mystery. They just seemed to appear one day down at your Nissen or dispersal and they generally adopted *you* rather than you adopt them! Of uncertain ancestry yours may have been, but you could not have wished for a better companion. You groundcrews, too, had your pets and all of you can smile at the memory of rolling about, helpless, laughing at the antics performed by the Billy goat distinctly under the influence of alcohol down on the village green;

or the amazing sight of a cockerel transfixed to the spot, unable to move its beak from a line of white chalk drawn on the floor of the farmhouse kitchen. Simple memories, yet meaningful at the time.

These are just two delightful reminders to illustrate man's best friend in war and peace. (84) An unknown crew (believed from No 625 Squadron Kelstern) display their pride and joy. Who are they? Did they survive?   *P. H. Miller*

(85) A certain well-known Labrador full of the joys of spring among the buttercups at Coningsby, May 1942. Behind Nigger, is Lanc 1 R5676 'ZN:E', among the first of the type received by No 106 Squadron and which would break up in the air under strange circumstances 12 February 1943 when with No 1660 HCU Swinderby. At the time of the picture Coningsby, like most other bomber airfields, was all grass.   *P. Cartwright*

86, 87   A Very Fine Car was the Austin. Your own aeroplane and car; what more could any youngster wish for! If you forget the dark side of the war, as you have as the years pass and the autumn of life approaches, you have cherished memories of many a pleasing hour spent breezing into town in the crew's japoly. You knew how precious your car was; few of you could afford to run a car let alone own one; and, of course, you were very popular with everyone at a time when most had to struggle with fixed-wheel bikes, or at best pack into a bus distinctly lacking good springs. On evenings when you were not flying, your crew, all seven of you, would cram into the Austin, Riley, even perhaps a Morgan Sports. Seems incredible now but in those days you weighed in at a lithe 10 stones dripping wet! It worried you little that a licence was required, while who drove back to camp tended to be he who was *less* inebriated! To civilians making-do in a nation totally geared for war, you were flamboyant, forever boisterous, singing your heads off as you meandered from one pub or dance hall to the next. So you got tanked up and made lots of noise! You had much on your mind, a pressure impossible to gauge, and you needed an escape valve. Unless you had bequeathed it to a pal in another crew, your car would be auctioned in the mess, the proceeds sent to your family should you go missing. What an ending.

These examples of men with their cars and kites show: (86) a September 1943 setting at Ludford Magna, with Flt Lt Bill ('Scrym') Scrymgeour-Wedderburn and his No 101 Squadron crew pausing awhile as their BIII, W4995 'SR:N' is readied for the night ahead; (87) BIII PB179 '60:Z' adding scale to the Austin Ruby owned by Flg Off Frank Lloyd and crew during their tour with No 582 Squadron, Little Staughton. The picture was taken either before Castrop Rauxel 21-22 November 1944 or a daylight to Heimbach Dam 3 December of the same year. In the event crews, aircraft and cars here illustrated survived the European War. W4995 was to crash at Lindholme, 16 May 1945, never to fly again; PB179 would be converted to ASRIII standard and live on until she crashed with 236 OCU, 29 January 1948.
W. A. Scrymgeour-Wedderburn; F. Lloyd

88   On the Warpath. Surrounded as you were by the echoes and constant reminders of war, you forever searched for some light relief. You needed little excuse to blur your fears and anxieties and shut out all that tomorrow might hold by exercising your gullet at the local hostelry, or taking a whirl around the dance floor with some delightful female companion. Nights-in at your camp could be lively too. Behind the hallowed walls of your mess was your one chance to really let your hair down, even if more staid admin types tended to frown on such hitherto unheard of behaviour. All this was, of course, unknown to the world at large, who saw only the image portrayed in feature films, or clipped footage on newsreels screened in cinemas. Were you from Canada, New Zealand and other distant lands, you did find yourself more in the public eye. Being far from the scene of action, your folks back home were eager for news of what you did, how you lived, any scrap of gen you cared to share. And so, features about you men and women at the war front were widely read — like this unusual 'ceremony' at Croft, 13 November 1944. Occasion was the naming of a Lanc X *Simcoe Warrior II* in honour of the town of Simcoe which 'adopted' No 431 ('Iroquois') squadron RCAF. CO Wg Cdr Eric Mitchell RCAF joins in the fun as eight of his girls perform an Iroquois war dance. (The original *Simcoe Warrior* was a Halifax III, which type equipped the squadron until October 1944.)
Public Archives of Canada

89

90

89, 90 Open and Welcome. When it was all over and peace again reigned, there was time to draw breath, time to take stock and begin to adjust. This, too, applied to you civilians. For six long years you had quietly supported the boys in blue by manning the machines of industry, supplying the means by which they carried out the distasteful job they had to do, and had accepted them in your midst. In all that time you rarely complained as you queued daily for the bare essentials of life, and were directed near and far by a Ministry of Production single-minded in its determination to keep the nation totally geared for a war it had to win at all costs. It would take years to adjust to a Lincoln, Nottingham or Cambridge strangely quiet, devoid of uniforms and voices from many lands. During those years you actually knew little of what really went on at your local Lancaster station and you accepted eagerly when its gates were thrown open soon after VE-day. It was an eye-opener indeed, just as it must have been for the Mayor and Mayoress of Lincoln, here (89) being shown around Polish-manned Faldingworth. Among the array of equipment assembled for inspection are incendiary clusters (foreground), Lancaster wing fuel tanks and nose section. (90) On the same occasion their Worships were treated to some vivid low-level flying by a trio of No 300 ('Masovian') Squadron's Lancasters. *Both: Polish Sources*

91 Tears of Memory. A few fading snapshots such as this, glued into a now rather ragged album, are all that many of you have to remind you of a heady past. As you occasionally feel the need to pull out the old album, maybe your dog-eared flying log book too, you retreat from the world about you. As you sit and let your mind wander, a thousand glimpses of your past crowd your head. It is at once disturbing and yet rewarding as the ghosts of men long-departed float before you, mere glimpses in your mind's eye, appearing as though in some kind of space bubble. As quickly as one image is there, it is gone . . . forced out by another . . . and another . . . each a glimpse of human agony and endeavour, of fortitude and guts . . . any one of a dozen facets of human experience war brings to the fore. You had known your fellow man in a way you never would again. You had seen the cool courage of a crew continuing their bombing run, unwavering as their Lancaster blazed from end to end, before plummeting earthwards like a falling

star, its gunners still spitting defiance at their tormentor, soon to be their victor. There were men who showed the strain and fear in their eyes but who kept going, knowing the odds were stacked against them. You knew men who were air-sick on every flight, others who would quietly pray by their beds each night . . . the visions are many . . . golden memories, sad memories . . . memories you find it impossible to share with even those now near to you. You close the album . . . your eyes are misting over.

Happily, the six No 433 ('Porcupine') Squadron RCAF crew men here seated in the grass at Skipton-on-Swale, spring 1945, would see the war out. Skipper Flt Lt Wally Pethick, third left, would return to his native Canada, and his crew disperse. Their Lanc, BI RA506 'BM:O', dubbed *Oboe*, would pass to No 427 ('Lion') Squadron RCAF at Leeming when 433 folded on 15 October 1945. Her end came in the huge Lancaster graveyard at No 20 MU, Aston Down, during May 1947. *L. W. Pethick*

91

65

What a Fright

Tom Matthews

Not all the action and excitement occurred on actual operations by any means. Every phase of flying carried its risks, right through from primary training to ops themselves. Before even reaching a squadron some crews had had more 'dicey do's' than others would experience on a whole tour. Whilst there could be no doubt that inexperience — and in some cases inability — played a part, other factors worked for or against you, depending on which way the finger of fate happened to be pointing. Accident prone; bad luck; mechanical failure; over enthusiasm? There was no standard 'cause and effect'.

Two widely differing stories of crews on almost identical cross-country training flights, both over the English Channel, illustrate what could happen — almost unbelievable if you didn't have six others to veryify the event; and showing how relaxed routine could turn suddenly to shock and fear, bringing out the best — or worst — in men.

First, an account by a rear gunner of a most unusual occurrence on a training flight. Sgt Tom Matthews, from Nottinghamshire, had already done one operation prior to the flight described, a mining stooge to the Bay of Biscay on the night of 20/21 June 1943 with Sgt L. F. Jeffries and crew. On this particular evening, however, he was with what was to be his regular crew, all RAFVR — Pilot, Flg Off W. F. (Wally) Snell; Nav, G. G. H. (George/'Doc') Russell; F/E, Les Heath; W/Op, Ivor J. Copping; B/A, Don E. Braybrook; M/U, Reg Bennett; R/G, Tom Matthews.

'23 June 1943. Normal morning — wash, dress, breakfast in the mess, then a casual walk down to the gunnery office. The only thing on the board was a DI (daily inspection) on one of the Lancs. As we were a new crew and I being the only member to have been on an "op", we didn't have a kite of our own so had to do DIs on any kite whose crew were on leave. Didn't take long to check: turret, guns and ammunition.

'Hung around talking to the ground crew till the NAAFI wagon arrived, then had char and wads all round. One or two of the old people from the village were walking along the footpath which ran by the dispersals. They told us that there would be no ops on as "things were not moving". By lunch time if you went into the local pub some of the old lads of the village could tell you the bomb load and fairly accurately the petrol load and could tell you if it would be a short trip or an all-night job! On the way to the mess met the skipper who told us that we were on a cross-country at night. All good experience.

'We all met in the crew room about 18.00hrs except for Reg (mid-upper gunner) who was on compassionate leave. We were told we didn't need another gunner where we were going. In Lanc III LM301 we took off at 19.05hrs and set course for Wales. I had a map and settled down to a bit of map reading. It was a lovely evening, only small puffs of cloud and brilliant sunshine.

'As we crossed Devon, Ivor (wireless op) called me up to ask if I'd like a cup of coffee. Never having been known to refuse, I came out of my turret and walked up the fuselage. On the way I climbed into the mid-upper turret (first time in a Lanc), had a look round and tried the controls and decided the rear turret was for me (you can't see the wings flap from there!). After a while I joined Ivor and as we drank coffee we listened to dance music on the radio.

'As time passed I heard Wally talking about Lands End just in front of us — when he suddenly asked me what the two fighters were off our port wing. I looked out of the astrodrome and nearly died of fright. Formating on our wing were a Focke-Wulf FW190 and a Messerschmitt Bf109! Panic!

'I dashed to the mid-upper turret and started loading the guns (no need to take another gunner so no need to load any guns). I was just loading the second gun when Ivor grabbed my leg and told me to go to the rear turret and he would use the mid-upper.

'I took another look at the two fighters. Both pilots were watching us. They were so close you could see their features clearly.

'After running to the rear turret two miles away (or so it seemed), although I couldn't see anything of the fighters, I quickly loaded up and started an all-round search — when all of a sudden gun-fire!

'On enquiring who had fired, the bomb aimer (Bray) said he was just testing his guns. Ivor said, as he had loaded the other gun, both fighters had dived down out of view.

'For the rest of the flight I never moved from my turret but kept an all-round search all the way back to base.

'On the way back we agreed that as we were in an isolated area, with no other planes in view, we would keep quiet about the whole incident and say nothing.

'It came as quite a shock when on joining the Wickenby circuit the Controller gave us permission to land with instructions to report to the watch office after parking the plane. The ideas of excuses were unlimited, but we decided to brazen the whole thing out. Apparently we had been plotted all round

the cross-country by the Observer Corps and were the only British plane in the area when a Fw190 crashed off Lands End. After a reprimand we went back to the mess for a meal, then off to bed about 1.30 determined to forget the matter for good.

'It was reported that on the next day on DROs (Daily Routine Orders) a reference was made to the fact that a FW190 crashed at Falmouth, out of control after being frightened by a Lancaster of 12 Squadron!'

The full Snell crew operated for the first time five nights later to Cologne, completing a full tour in a week under six months. Wally Snell, Don Braybrook and Doc Russell were awarded DFCs, Ivor Copping and Tom Matthews DFMs. The crew with which Tom did his first op were lost on a raid to Gelsenkirchen 9/10 July 1943.

LM301 had a long career, passing to Nos 100 and 550 Squadrons before going down on a Berlin op, 2/3 December 1943 . . . just another mere statistic for the archives.

92 Tail with a Sting. Sgt Tom Matthews in the rear turret of a No 12 Squadron Lanc. Note central Perspex panel removed for clearer vision. *T. Matthews*

What are the Odds a Third Time?

Ted Robbins and George Calvert

The second story concerns another (coincidentally) all-British crew, which suffered a trio of incidents, the first two of which could have daunted lesser men. They pressed on, however, and were well into their tour of ops when the third, and final, crash-landing ended their operational career. Thanks to a considerable degree of discipline and skill, they escaped with their lives, but could so easily have been remembered as mere entries in the record books: 'unexplained fatal accident'; or just plain 'FTR'.

Sgt E. A. (Ted) Robbins was only 19 years old when posted to No 19 OTU Kinloss, on the Moray Firth in November 1942, crewing up with another bunch of lads of similar

age, all fresh out of basic training. Ted was English, but had spent some years in Canada before the war. He joined up in England, but did his flying training in the USA.

After 25 hours of day flying on Whitleys, the training switched to night flying exercises: bombing practice, cross-countries, photo flashes, loop bearings, QDMs etc. On 9 December 1942, the crew took off in Whitley 'T — Tommy' for a night cross-country at 16.45. It was already pitch dark, with strong winds and snow flurries adding their own dimension to the testing of still inexperienced airmen.

Soon after climb-out the port engine caught fire and had to be shut down, and the Whitley turned for home. It was found that the wheels and flaps would not lower, due to loss of services from the dead engine. In worsening weather conditions, the crew found the airfield's dimly-lit runway and in a strong crosswind, Ted Robbins demonstrated the utmost skill in making a perfect belly landing, coming to rest only a hose

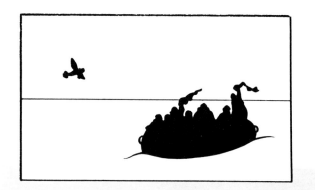

93, 94 Reward for Survival. To the Robbins' crew, the minesweeper *Ewald* was a lovely sight. Whatever became of her? How many men can show you a Goldfish and bar brevet! This one belongs to W/op George Calvert. *Both: G. Calvert*

93

length away from the waiting fire tenders. The only slight injury — the W/Op bruised his knee on his table when the aircraft touched down.

Already the crew had cause to thank their skipper for his coolness and skill.

Less than three hours later they were airborne again in another Whitley for an hour's local flying just to ensure they hadn't lost their nerve or appetite for flying. The RAF did not believe in letting men's minds dwell on fright for long!

On completing the OTU course, and after enjoying a spot of Christmas leave, the crew re-mustered at their new posting, No 1661 Conversion Unit at Winthorpe. There they were teamed-up with a flight engineer and mid-upper gunner, who made up the full complement of seven, most of them only 18 or 19, all sergeants. The crew was: Pilot, E. A. (Ted) Robbins; F/E, John Seedhouse; B/A, Les Calvert; Nav, Les Carpenter; W/Op, George Calvert; M/U, H. (Bert) Manley; R/G, Jack Denton. (The two Calverts were not related.)

On 9 January 1943 came their first flight together as a complete crew — in Manchester R5838, and after 15 hours on type, they finally got to fly the aircraft of their choice — the Lancaster, when, on 8 February, Ted flew them in R5547 on a 1½-hour local conversion trip.

There followed two weeks of intensive familiarisation training, being airborne every day until, having done 12½ hours, and having more-or-less mastered the complexities of the Lanc, came the big moment — off on their own without

instructors for the first time, on a cross-country, a major stepping stone on the course, and in their career as a crew. It represented a culmination stage in their training.

On 21 February they took off at 11.20am in Lancaster R5892, loaded with eight sand-filled 1,000lb bombs to give them the feel of the aircraft with an operational load. They had been briefed to drop two of the bombs at each of four practice ranges dotted round the English and Welsh coast, and which would be their en-route turning points, the first being in the The Wash. From there they headed south to drop two more bombs on The Naze, before turning southwest for the next objective, just off Lands End.

This was to be the longest leg of the flight, and they were soon high above the forecasted layer of unbroken cloud moving in from the west, climbing steadily in brilliant sunshine, nearing their intended ceiling of 20,000ft, in the vicinity of Reading.

The W/Op, George Calvert takes up the story:

'Everything was going well, each member of the crew thoroughly enjoying himself, getting to know each other. Two hours out and the wireless was working perfectly. I had tuned-in to some pleasant dance music for relaxation, and I was warm and comfortable.

'Then suddenly, everything changed.

'There was an almighty bang, as if the Lanc had received a near miss from flak. It immediately plunged into a very steep spiral dive — virtually a spin — from which no-one thought it would recover. We'd never experienced anything like it before. Looking out through the window opposite my seat, I could see the starboard inner engine had lost its cowlings, and the wing leading edge had disappeared right back to the wing root; a lot of skin from the top surface of the wing had also gone, and it was fortunate none had hit the tailplane or fins. All four engines were going full blast.

'Slowly, Ted, aided by the flight engineer, regained control, and by their combined efforts on the control wheel, gradually pulled the aircraft out of its dive, in which we lost some 6,000ft. On Ted's instructions I contacted our home base to report what had happened. We were advised to head for Manston, which had a huge runway specially provided for such emergencies. Manston offered advice on speeds, etc, and gave a heading to steer, but we were losing height, and wouldn't make it; and in any case, it was found that the speed required to prevent the Lanc stalling was too high, even for Manston.

'Closer examination of the starboard undercarriage revealed that not only was the tyre flat, but also one of the legs was bent upwards at a 30deg angle. So Ted decided the only thing to do was put her down on the sea, and this was relayed to both base and Manston Control before heading out towards the Channel at 160mph, which was judged to be the best speed for maintaining a degree of stability and control. A lucky cloud break revealed the sea below, and enabled us to jettison the remaining dummy bombs, thus relieving us of one problem.

'The crew set about ditching preparations. Our training was to be put to the test. I concentrated on sending a Mayday distress call, first ensuring the trailing aerial was out, and the correct "South Coast MF/DF" frequencies selected. There was a lot of Morse on the air, but it immediately ceased once the SOS had been tapped out, and suddenly, I had the frequency all to myself, a tribute to the high standard of RAF discipline.

'It was comforting to receive a response, and confirmation that bearings had been taken, with approximate position given. Our nav had also worked out our position which I transmitted back to the ground station. The routines were operating splendidly.

'By this time the Lanc was low over the sea, and we were warned by our skipper to take up crash positions, so I clamped down the Morse key and crouched against the wing root bulkhead. We hit the sea with a great bump, and water gushed rapidly into the fuselage, the aircraft soon coming to a halt. I pulled the cord on the inside of the fuselage to inflate the dinghy, and we pushed off the escape hatches on top of the fuselage.

'On my way out I picked up the Very pistol and a couple of cartridges, and struggled through the hatch to see the dinghy inflating — a welcome sight. Ted was scrambling along the top of the cockpit, and by this time the Lanc was already beginning to sink nose down. The sea must have flooded in quickly through the damaged starboard wing.

'Six of us got into the dinghy relatively easily, stepping-in without even getting wet, but poor Bert Manley, the mid-upper gunner, was in the sea in full Irvin suit and flying gear, already very heavy. We had difficulty pulling him aboard, and only managed it after a struggle. The aircraft was sinking rapidly, and we cut loose the tethering rope.

'The Lanc suddenly plunged nose down, followed by its tail section which had broken off on impact, the twin fins disappearing like the tail of a great whale. We estimated she had been on the surface $2\frac{1}{2}$ minutes at most.

'There was a lot of jagged debris floating about, which we gingerly pushed away from our dinghy in case it got punctured. There was a gentle swell, at the top of which we could just see what we were fairly sure was our coastline on the horizon. After checking our Mae Wests and other bits and pieces of equipment and stores we started to paddle, somewhat hopefully.

'Already, I think we were grateful for all the dinghy drill we had done in training, and which, at times, had seemed something of a chore.

'We felt quite elated, and considered we had come out of it all rather well so far, with no injuries. We began to discuss what had happened, when we might be picked up, and by whom. Being in mid-Channel, it could be either side we reckoned. At least we had the satisfaction of knowing someone knew we were down, our distress call having been positively acknowledged.

'We hadn't been in the dinghy long when suddenly three fighters were coming straight for us at low level in a "vic", looking very like FW190s head-on. Several of us prepared to dive into the sea, fearing a machine gun attack. The fighters banked steeply round us and with relief were identified as Typhoons, a type fairly new to us. Two of them maintained a protective orbit overhead while the third made off towards the coast, reappearing in our direction several times, obviously acting as a guide.

'Before long, we saw a column of smoke on the horizon, and thought it a good idea to fire a Very cartridge, following which we watched the direction of the vessel. After a while, there was no doubt it was heading our way, so we fired our other cartridge. Someone was definitely coming for us!

'Soon we could see its outline, and it grew into a small ship, which eventually stopped 100 yards or so away. Quite a few sailors lined the deckrail, their uniforms unfamiliar to our eyes, and looking German-like. A large man with a big red beard, and who we guessed was the Captain, bellowed out: "Are you English?" Not knowing any other language, we could only answer — "Yes, we're English". What would be his reaction to this? Several of the sailors had rifles. The answer really surprised us: "OK — We Dutch". We paddled alongside and were hauled aboard along with our dinghy; and were now in very high spirits; lots of back slapping. We noticed the rifles being stowed away and I don't think German aircrew would have got quite the same reception.

95, 96 **Best of British.** How many of you posed for 'mug shots' like these? (95) Skipper Ted Robbins, home from The States, as yet unsoiled wings on his chest. (96) The folks at home liked to see you in your 'operational' gear, too. George Calvert, who, like most W/ops, rarely needed to 'dress up' for ops. His station in the Lancaster was where the hot air came out.
G. Calvert; E. A. Robbins

'The ship was a minesweeper — HM *Ewald* of the Klondyke Marine, formerly from Rotterdam. "Capt Red Beard" told us he was heading for Portland Bill. Our luck was holding. Our wet clothes and flying boots were taken down to the engine room to dry. We agreed to let the crew have our flying boots, and in exchange they gave us various items of footwear. I received a pair of gaily-painted wooden clogs, which I still have to this day.

'Until this moment, I had never seen skipper Ted smoke or touch alcohol; but here he was now with a cigarette in his mouth, mug of coffee in one hand, a cognac in the other, with the rest of us! The Dutch crew were a happy crowd; we didn't envy them their job.

'We heard the sound of aircraft engines, and again wondered what we were in for. The plane was soon identified as an Air-Sea Rescue Walrus. It made a few low passes and headed for home. No doubt now as to our whereabouts and position being known. Shortly afterwards, a RN ASR launch

came speeding our way, and its Captain tannoyed for details of how many airmen picked up, and destination, etc. He decided not to transfer the seven of us, but to escort us into Portland. We were being so well looked after, and were quite content to remain with the Dutch crew. On arrival at Portland, and after thanks all round, we were taken to the Naval hospital for a bath and a short medical at which we were all pronounced fit and well. I was still wearing my newly-won clogs which were clumsy and awfully noisy. We were then taken to the ASR base at Warmwell for debriefing, this being where the launch had come from, and where our SOS had been picked up.

'We also learned that an Army colonel, who had been walking along a cliff top, had actually seen us come down a few miles off St Albans Head, and had immediately reported it. So, we had many things going in our favour on that day.

'We returned to Newark by train, a rather motley looking bunch, and me in my clogs. At King's Cross station we were stopped by MPs who talked about putting us on a charge because of our appearanice. We felt we had earned the week's survivors' leave which we were eventually given.'

At the Court of Enquiry held into the loss of the aircraft, the pilot and flight engineer were made to stand to attention for $1\frac{3}{4}$ hours while questions were fired at them. The theory eventually reached and accepted was that the starboard tyre had burst. The pilot and crew were highly praised for their actions. They had earned their Goldfish Club brevets.

In mid-March 1943, the crew joined No 106 Squadron at Syerston and on 28 March, flew its first op — to St Nazaire in Lanc W4156. Within two months they had done a total of 16, all night ops, some to distant targets such as Spezia on 18/19 April, a long 'flog' of over 10 hours in W4842. They had their moments: coned by searchlight for eight minutes over Stettin; a flak hole in the bomb aimer's compartment over Pilsen; an engine knocked out over Duisberg. But always, Ted and the Lanc had brought them home.

Their luck (but not their skill) was to finally run out on the night of 27/28 May 1943, a night on which they need not have operated, as the mid-upper gunner, Bert Manley, had reported sick with a throat infection. Ted Robbins, keen to go, asked the CO of No 106 Squadron (Wg Cdr Baxter) for a spare mid-upper. The Wing Commander was not flying that night, so offered the services of his own regular mid-upper, 'Spud' Taylor, which was accepted.

Over Krupps of Essen, the most hotly defended of all targets, their faithful W4842, 'ZN-H' received a direct hit by flak immediately after 'bombs gone'. Again a very steep dive, this time with both port engines on fire, and in a pitch dark enemy sky, Ted Robbins fighting to pull the Lanc out of her plunge, eventually doing so at 5,000ft, and with another stricken bird on his hands.

The fire extinguishers doused the flames, there were no injuries to the crew, and there seemed a chance they could make it. The Lanc was shaking severely, and the bomb doors were found to have jammed open; these and the cavernous bomb bay creating enormous drag and turbulence. Suddenly the starboard-inner burst into flames, but the fire died when the engine was shut down, leaving the Graviner in reserve in case there was a chance of restarting it.

One good engine left working at full bore — the starboard-outer. Even with full trim wound on, it took both feet on the right rudder to counter the pull of the one motor. The crew declined to bale out, and elected to take their chance. Every possible item went overboard: guns, ammo, bomb sight, spare flares; even the ladder so as to lighten the load. Despite this the Lanc was still slowly losing height and turning left, fighting a losing battle with the drag of three dead engines and the open bomb bay. The starboard-inner engine was restarted, but immediately burst into flames again, having to

be feathered and the extinguisher used. The fate of 'ZN-H' was now sealed. Down to only 3,000ft, and with little chance of now making even the North Sea, let alone England. The trailing aerial had been shot away, so no chance either of another SOS signal even if they were to ditch.

Their gently curving track took them directly over the middle of Amsterdam, where they became a sitting target for what seemed like every searchlight and AA gun in the city. The crew, from their crash positions, saw tracers pass right through the holes in the fuselage, yet they somehow got through unscathed. The landing lights were switched on, partly in the hope that it might signify a 'defenceless' situation to the enemy gunners, a ruse recently employed by cripped German aircraft over England.

On the assumption they must now be near the coast, or the Zuider Zee, the pilot eased the nose down, hoping to see something in the beam of the landing lamp. He did — a church steeple or windmill sail, and the Lanc almost stalled as he immediately pulled up to avoid it. Then, suddenly, the glint of water ahead, she was eased down, skipped a couple of times on the surface, flopped on to a muddy island and slithered to a halt, coming to rest in dead silence. Ted had pulled off yet another copybook belly landing. The time was 01.59hrs.

Within two days all the crew had been taken prisoner. For them the war was over.

Today, six of them still survive, one having died in recent years. As George Calvert says: 'We owe so much to Ted Robbins'.

By an amazing coincidence, the Dutchman who owns the garden centre in Hertfordshire where Ted works, lived in 1943 in the village of Sassenheim, near Warmond. Mr Cornelius Van Hage recalls clearly the night a Lancaster passed over his parents' house at little more than roof-top level, narrowly missing the nearby church steeple; and the next day, going to see the plane on the small island — Ted Robbins' Lanc. It was not until 1980 that this coincidence was discovered.

97 No Hiding Place. The locals take a look at B1 W4842 'ZN:H' a day or so after Ted Robbins put her down on the island near Warmond. No amount of effort by the crew could destroy her. When the destructive devices failed to work, they fired off the Very pistols — to no avail. In their haste to get away they forgot the pigeons, so B/A and W/op returned. Bomb aimer Les Calvert then wrote a message and put it in one of the leg rings before releasing the two birds — and never did find out if they delivered it!
G. Zijlstra via E. A. Robbins

A Action

98

Where Pulse the Arteries of War

The nervous conversation dies,
The curtains part,
Eliciting a gasp of shocked surprise
As, reaching out across the sprawling chart,
The crazy zig-zag of the tortuous thread
Squeezing between the fighters and the flak,
Marks out the fire-torn route ahead
That we must follow out;
And, given luck, trace back.

Philip A. Nicholson

98 Night Must fall. Above: the scudding clouds as though racing against the oncoming night; below: the myriad airfields spread throughout fertile Lincolnshire appear as gigantic pools of diffused light; at their dispersals the Lancasters of Bomber Command take on an ever darkening and menacing shape in the fast gathering gloom. It is that time when all that has to be done before an operation has been done; at other than the odd dispersal the bombing-up and fuelling is finished and the F700s have been signed. Your tasks are complete; all but a few of you have filtered away, either to partake of cookhouse delights, or to linger awhile in your own 'private' huts beside each hardstand. This prelude lasts perhaps an hour before the crew buses disgorge their load of noisy, boisterous aircrew . . . .

An 'Airborne Cigar'-equipped Lanc of No 101 Squadron pictured at Ludford Magna (the two top-fuselage-mounted aerials can just be discerned). *V. Redfern*

73

99, 100   Likely Lads. The crew room is the usual babble of noise
and disarray. The air is filled with brisk chatter and convulsive
mirth, if a little forced, with periodic interruptions when you cannot
prise open your locker or someone finds his gloves or scarf have
been 'half inched'. Everywhere is a jumble of parachutes and
helmets and boots and men struggling into unwieldy flying gear. As
a crew fresh to the fray you chatter and fidget nervously, your
heads buzzing with a confusion of hopes and fears, mentally
discounting the many rumours with you, ever since OTU days,
remembering all you have been taught. As an older, established
crew, you know your way round the unlit skies of Europe almost as
well as you know your own home town; you are more subdued;
you have seen it all before and seem somehow more relaxed —
almost nonchalant and remote — yet you are a team through and
through, lacking nothing in efficiency and dedication.

(99) Aussie Plt Off Geoff Tillotson and his No 467 Squadron
RAAF crew preparing for Berlin in the Bottesford locker room
early in 1943, giving us a clear view of a bomber crew's range of
impedimenta for the period. This is a crew building itself a fine
record; they will survive their tour. *Mrs M. Claridge Collection*

(100) A delightful study of No 101 Squadron air gunners
'hanging around' in the crew room (again the ubiquitous Nissen
hut) at Ludford Magna, awaiting the crew buses and trucks before
yet another trip to Berlin (20-21 January 1944). Handing out those
well remembered slabs of Fry's Sandwich chocolate is Londoner
Sgt Percy Drought, mid-upper in the crew skippered by Flt Lt Roy
Leeder. About to receive his ration is his rear gunner Sgt Eric
Bickley and both wear the bright yellow Taylor suit with built-in
heating elements and typical clobber of the day. They, too, will
survive while several familiar faces in the background are those of
ghosts — men whose luck will run out in the blood-soaked night
skies yet whose names will live on in the pages of No 1 Group's
Roll of Honour residing in Lincoln Cathedral, there for evermore.
D. Hall

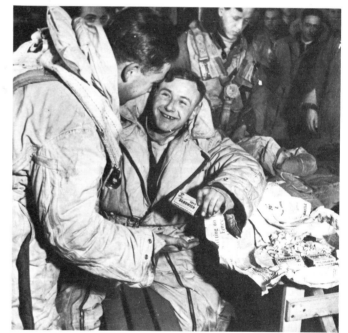

101 Twilight Thunder. Against a backdrop of swirling clouds and fading light a No 83 Squadron Lanc is run up at Scampton circa mid-1942.

There is still one hour before take-off and all around the airfield Merlins are winding up as you run through your individual checks. The earth trembles underfoot, reverberating to the confusion of rising and falling engine tones as you pilots and engineers in two dozen dimmed cockpits play throttle and pitch levers to run each Merlin in turn through its full power range, until satisfied boost settings and magneto levels are in order. Outside, your patient groundcrews who have laboured all day can but stand aside, their task complete, and trust there are no last minute snags. For you aircrew that 'gut' feeling which began early morning on learning you were 'on' tonight, now begins to recede, as within your world of metal, dope and rubber — an undefinable tangy, slightly nauseating odour peculiar to aircraft — you are busy checking and re-checking . . . . *G. E. Fawke*

102 Easy on the Brakes. Moments before, BIII PB509 'OJ:C' of No 149 (East India) Squadron stood silent at tree-lined Methwold . . . silent that is save for the odd creak and groan, as of an old house asleep; but asleep she is not for within her cramped and cluttered interior you are at work, preparing mentally and physically for the hours which lie ahead. Now, her motors running, she is alive, soon to shake free the earth her temporary master, soon to rise and fall in her natural element. The roar of those superb thoroughbred Merlins sends waves of power pulsing through your kite, wearing away an overpowering sense of foreboding hitherto flooding your mind; so, too, the anxieties gnawing within you since seeing your crew listed on the battle order will largely dissolve once airborne. With work to do, running through your checks for the umpteenth time, the icy twinge in your stomach recedes. Your actions are mechanical, your mind focused wholly on the task ahead, excluding all else about you. Next, your skipper opens the outboard throttles wide for a moment, then closes them, to set the Lanc in motion, leaving behind you a swirling cloud of dust or spray, the friendly faces of your groundcrew. (PB509 would pass to neighbouring No 186 Squadron at Stradishall and ultimately succumb to the breakers at No 22 MU, Silloth, December 1945.) *M. E. Staves*

102

103 Quick and Slow. What an impressive sight it was to witness your squadron's Lancasters waddling round the perimeter track prior to take-off. The cacophony of sound was deafening to the ear, the raucous tones of up to 100 Merlins interrupted by frequent hisses and squeals from protesting brakes as you checked your charge so as not to run into the Lanc ahead. A Lanc would taxi at something like 30mph and you would be keeping a watchful eye on engine temperatures, for Merlins running at little more than idling speed could soon 'boil' if there was undue delay; the odd burst of power was necessary in order to avoid oiling up the plugs. As groundcrew, were you on hand to marshal your kite into dispersal on return from the night's outing, you, too, had to be alert. A lumbering Lancaster coming at you as you walked backwards, half-blinded by the bomb aimer's Aldis piercing the lashing rain or swirling mist was quite frightening. Your pulse dropped only when the skipper had her in position and shut down. Here we have No 463 Squadron RAAF Lancs threading their way round Waddo's peri-track before setting off for Munich, 24-25 April 1944. Nearest kite is BI LL844 'JO:R', dubbed *Ginger Megs* and flown by Sqn Ldr Bill Brill RAAF and crew. In the event her career was to be long, her operational tally reaching 72 before 'retirement' and seeing the war out at No 46 MU Lossiemouth for eventual scrapping (January 1947). Escaping the wartime censor, we can see Waddington's fenced-off bomb dump beside the Lincoln-Sleaford road. *R. A. Buckham Collection*

103

104, 105 Bogged. You found negotiating winding, dimly lit perimeter tracks far from easy. Even in daylight, in ideal conditions, it required careful handling to avoid a mainwheel and tyre running over the concrete's edge and digging in to the soft earth, be it dry or covered in mud or slush. At night, sitting some 15ft up, your view greatly restricted by the bulk of the mainplane, you needed all your wits about you. Aided by your bomb aimer down in the nose, shining his Aldis as appropriate, and your engineer up with you in the cockpit as an extra pair of eyes, you needed to keep a careful watch on the aircraft in front. On the other hand, if a mishap befell those ahead of you, you might be forced to apply engine power (rudders being ineffective at such slow speed) and veer off the peri-track to avoid a collision. You faced an anxious time while ground staff tugged and pushed, their curses clearly audible above the revving engines of half-track or bowser straining to drag you out. Shown is No 49 Squadron's BIII ED805 'EA:S' stuck fast at Fiskerton, her port wheel and tyre having broken through the concrete, 11 August 1943. One week later Sqn Ldr R. N. Todd-White and crew took her to Peenemunde, 17-18 August, and did not return. *Both: J. A. Edwards*

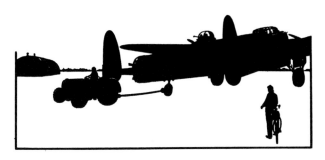

105

106 Soon the Darkness. Take-off: a medley of tension . . . excitement . . . and noise. Everything, everywhere, full of the sound of engines; the whole air dazed with power. A time when there seemed no other life than your line of aircraft, the caravan, the waiting knot of people. You doubtless stood in that line the very first day you arrived at your station. Eager as you were to complete the bind of reporting in at each and every section, you soon found yourself swept up in the tide of anticipation and fervour charging the air like an electric current as the station prepared for the impending op; and so you could not resist joining others of your kind at the runway's end as take-off neared. You watched, mesmerised, as the first Lanc rolled forward, slowly at first, the inertia of the bomb load making her sluggish, slow to react. Then, faster, gaining momentum, as you who were her skipper and engineer fed power to those howling Merlins. Inside the dimmed cockpit you would be watching like hawks for the first sign of a

swing, juggling with your outer engines, forcing the tail up to get rudder control. She would be pulling to port and you would need to kick the nose straight again. Soon you could feel her straining to fly, could feel the air plucking and pushing at her rudders and stiffening them under your feet, could sense the gift of flight pulsing through the palms of your hands. Maintaining a steady backward movement of the control column, you would feel her ease off the runway, reluctantly at first, her wheels briefly skipping the concrete a couple of times before shaking herself completely free and settling into the climb.

A No 61 Squadron Lanc preparing to flex her wings at Syerston, November 1943, destination . . . The Big City. The snap is notable for being taken inside a car (would that more of you were so enterprising), and for a lack of any WAAFs. But they will be somewhere near waving the boys off, their handkerchiefs fluttering like moths in the fading light. *H. N. Scott*

106

107 On the Wing. Lifting off Linton's main runway, this No 408 ('Goose') Squadron RCAF BII is at the 'point of no return'. It is that moment when you watch ever closer the dancing dials and gauges and your ears strain for the slightest hesitation in engine note. The noise is deafening, four Hercules at full power making speech impossible. The clock registers 110 and you breathe a slight, private sigh of relief as you are airborne and the great wings quite distinctly shudder and flutter under the cushion of air. In no time at all the nose dips a degree or two as the undercart comes up, tucks into each inner nacelle with a slight clump and is recorded on the cockpit panel by red lights winking out. Above 500ft the nose dips

again, more pronounced this time as the flaps come up in five-degree snatches and the skipper trims to compensate, by now sweating freely from sheer exertion, both physical and nervous. With the engineer then setting the revs to 2,850 the Lanc settles into a steady climb at 165mph and another operation has begun.

The picture affords a good view across Linton-on-Ouse, commissioned prewar and having massive brick-built hangars and attendant buildings. Keen eyes will spot two grounded BIIs, one lying on her belly, the other askew with one undercarriage collapsed. *R. J. Russell*

107

108 You and the Night. The urgency of take-off over, a No 35 (Madras Presidency) Squadron Lanc circles above a Graveley fast taking on a pattern of golden brown mistiness tinged with mauve, with here and there the blinking of marker beacons and airfield lights. Another day is dying, in its last throes of active life a glorious arena of gold and purple hues, vast and serene. Within the narrow, cramped confines of your Lancaster the sky appears totally empty; but they are there allright, those other creatures of the night, soon to hove into view as you all head for the turning point over Reading and untold dangers ahead. To those earth-bound mortals observing from below — from farm and garden, village and town alike — you appear as moths circling a dimming candle flame, ever higher . . . until the last steady, drumming note of Merlins recede and silent darkness overtakes the countryside. *K. C. Gooch*

108

109

109 Night Wings. Appearing ghost-like, almost akin to huge dragonflies, No 50 Squadron Lancasters, airborne from their native Skellingthorpe, point their blunt noses eastwards and head for the rendezvous. Where moments ago you felt you could well have been the only aircraft aloft this night, there appear, suddenly and seemingly from nowhere, a spawning horde of shadowy shapes, soon to reveal themselves as other Lancasters. While there is yet time to link up with one, maybe two of your fellow travellers, soon the winking navigation lights and periodic messages flashed by

Aldis from an astrodome will cease and you will settle down to the lonely tension-packed trip ahead.

Genuine pictures like this (snapped by bomb aimer Flt Sgt Les Bartlett during the winter of 1943/4, probably from BI LL744, 'VN:B', regular mount of Flg Off Mike Beetham and crew) are none too common. Apart from being 'actively discouraged' cameras and films of the day were a far cry from those available four decades later. *A. L. Bartlett*

110, 111 That Other World. Peering from behind cockpit and turret Perspex, your ears ringing to the roar of Hercules or Merlins, few of you could fail to appreciate the towering magnificence of nature's cloudscapes, golden sunsets and inspiring daybreaks. It seemed so unreal, sharing a peaceful silent world with an agent of destruction, and death never far away. For each of you it was all too easy to withdraw within yourself, forget your cramped position and become immersed in some kind of dream. At night in particular you could quickly be lost in a vast unending sea of darkening brown, turning to indigo, broken perhaps by some distant wavering stars — as if messengers with whom you felt more contact than with any of your kind . . . until you would be brought, sharply, back to reality.

(110) A view from a No 83 Squadron Lanc from Wyton or Coningsby en route to Germany in 1944 as the sun slowly sinks beyond the horizon and darkness fast approaches. *L. C. Deane*

(111) Clouds as far as the eye can see mask the bomber stream as it heads eastwards in daylight some months later. Bathed in sunlight, her wings, cockpit and turret Perspex reflecting the sun's rays, is the near-silhouetted 'JN:O' from 75 (New Zealand) Squadron's 'C' Flight, Mepal. Her extended bomb bay breaks an otherwise classic outline. Even the dihedral of the wing has become a graceful curve under the war load she bears. *S. H. Richmond*

111

Through Endless Seas of Cloud

Astern the straggling line of Lancs
Recedes to the horizon;
Below, the rolling fleece of cloud
Beguiles in its freshness;
But soon, as the bombs tumble
And smoke rises,
To smudge the whiteness,
The image dissolves and
We turn for home,
Uneasily aware of unseen destruction.

Philip A. Nicholson

113

112, 113 Gaggles. Around you, no matter which way you look, up or down, to port or starboard, there are fellow Lancasters. The stream is huge — rather like a gigantic snake meandering through the sky — each 'vic' of three Lancs continually changing position slightly relative to its neighbours as they strive to keep station; and, inevitably, there are the stragglers, both within and at the edge of the stream, who have temporarily lost their leader and tag on to another vic, or those whose aircraft find difficulty keeping up and steadily fall behind. You find the gaggle a comforting sight; it makes a welcome change from the loneliness of night operations — even if failure to judge the agitated slipstreams and vortices churned up by those in front is an added danger. Concentration is vital. Lack of it can quickly result in you being tossed into the path of another Lanc and there will be little chance of survival in the ensuing collision.

(112) A 3 Group gaggle heading for Bassens (Bordeaux) in daylight, 5 August 1944. Below them is the Bay of Biscay. Nearest the camera is No 622 Squadron's B1 LL802 'GI:M' flown by Flg Off Ted Orton and crew and who were destined to go down on Stuttgart, 19-20 October 1944. (LL802 met her end when she collided in cloud with B1 LM167, also from 622 Squadron, over Wormington, Essex, 20 September of the same year; the target that day was Calais.) *J. Humphreys*

(113) A 1 Group daylight effort late 1944/early 1945 and differing in composition when compared with the G-H vics adopted by 3 Group. Left foreground are the BABS/Eureka nose aerials of a No 12 Squadron Lanc. *R. C. Nash*

114 Your Move or Mine? The two gunners of this No 166 Squadron Lanc will be keeping a watchful eye on a sister machine from the same outfit (and from which this snapshot was taken) keeping station during a daylight. It will be an anxious time when in the target area, with the sky appearing full of raining bombs and jinking aircraft. A 1,000-pounder alone can tear off a wing like a knife slices through butter and when it does you stand little chance of extricating yourselves from the stricken bomber, which will immediately flick over in a vicious spin and subject you to centrifugal forces impossible to imagine. Even though Bomber Command's heavy brigade attacked in daylight as a gaggle rather than the tight box-formations operated by the 8th United States Army Air Force, the sky would appear somewhat crowded to you Lanc and Hally crews, frequently forced to side slip in order to find a safe gap.

Some will argue that on night ops ignorance was bliss in that you did not see other kites about you? Even so we shall never know how many crews went down due to cascading loads (among them, of course, 4,000lb 'Cookies') and collisions. Certainly you surviving crew men can testify to many a near miss! Depicted is No 166 Squadron's BI ME835 'AS:T' flown by Flg Off J. R. Wilson and crew and photographed from BI PD239 'AS:Z' by Norwegian Lt Hallvard Vikholt, doing his 'second dickey' with Flg Off Walter McElwain RNZAF and crew on Le Havre, 10 September 1944. McElwain and Vikholt were to complete their tours, but the Wilson crew went down (in ME835) on Bochum 4-5 November 1944. PD239 survived until a daylight on Emmerich, 7 October 1944. *H. Vikholt*

114

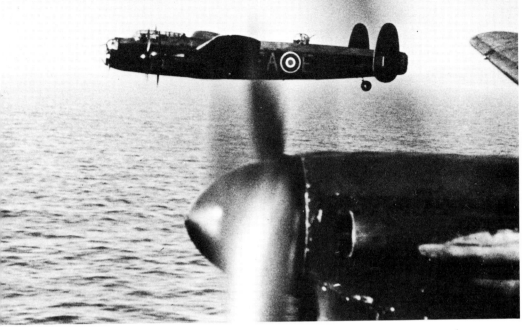

115-117 Close Companions. Either you revelled in formation flying or you disliked it intensely. For those who enjoyed the experience there were few more pleasing ways of passing a lazy day, a day free from anxiety and pressure when you knew you were not on the battle order. Mind you, even when two, three or more of you took your Lancs aloft intent on putting in some useful hours of G-H bombing practice, or learning to tighten up the gaggles, you could encounter problems. What might start out as a day of promise could quickly turn into one of terror should you run into towering cu nims and electrical storms, forcing you to disperse hurriedly. From soaking up the rays of a summer sun pouring down on you, forcing you to strip down to shirt sleeves, you could before long be sat huddled in near darkness, 'chutes clipped on, holding on tight while your Lanc was bucked and tossed so violently you thought her wings would come off. Many of you had your fill of formation flying long before you became operational. At every stage of your training you spent interminable hours flying hither and thither, and you were convinced your superiors had an obsession with the subject. It was only when at OTU and HCU it dawned on you how useful such stooges could be. If nothing else they taught you just what skill (and effort!) was required for any number of multi-engined heavies to keep station with one another, affording mutual protection, hour after hour, all the time keeping within the limits of economic cruising levels, getting the best out of your engines. Of course, were you doing your ops during 1942/3 you rarely ventured out in daylight in any case and would rarely, if ever again put this skill to use. You had to console yourself with seeing the war out instructing others while daily you looked longingly at the Lanc gaggles passing overhead . . . a paradox you never did understand; nor can you explain even now.

(115) Nose-up attitude of No 49 Squadron's B1 R5751 'EA:E' tells us skipper Sqn Ldr Eric Couch has her trimmers set right back with the unfriendly sea but a hiccup below. The squadron is in practise for Le Creusot, 17 October 1942, or a follow-up to Milan one week later on the 24th — both probing daylights by No 5 Group before winter sets in and puts paid to further efforts. (The Couch crew would leave Scampton tour-expired while R5751 would end up as instructional airframe 5257M following service with no less than five training units.) *L. C. Slee*

(116) No 195 Squadron crews from Wratting Common prove they are no slackers when it comes to formation flying.
J. H. Harper

(117) VE-Day 1945 presents No 617 Squadron with the opportunity of indulging in some light relief when they show off their wares over Lincoln. Up from Woodhall Spa are BI (Special) PD129 'YZ:O' and sister, PD118 'YZ:M', resplendent in 'day' finish, mixing it with near-standard B1 'KC:M' whose 'night' paintwork is in sharp contrast. *S. J. Venton*

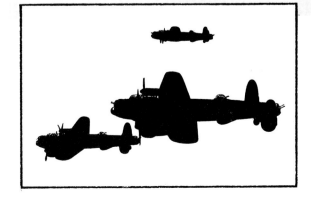

118 Cloud Companions. Were you in PFF, flying from Oakington or Graveley, Upwood or Gransden Lodge, Downham Market or Little Staughton, there is every chance you got to know the Mossie boys who shared your 'drome. As much as you Lanc types kept to yourselves, there can surely be few among you who did not wangle a flip in one of the wooden wonders. What an experience! As much as you loved your Lancs, you had to concede a few points to the little fellows, who forever managed to take-off one hour behind you, yet could invariably get back an hour before you! A good deal of ribbing resulted over that whenever your two squadrons met up at a station dance, or rubbed shoulders in drinking haunts like 'The Beehive' at Eltisley (if based at Graveley), or any one of a dozen pubs in Cambridge. Sometimes the laugh was on them when Group decided you must operate together. Were you with No 582 Squadron at Little Staughton, some of your Lancs had Oboe radar fitted and you sometimes flew with No 109 Squadron's Mossie navigators in your crew or one of their pilots driving your Lanc. Some of them died with you, too . . . like Sqn Ldr Robert Palmer, who went down as skipper of a 582 Lancaster on the memorable daylight to Cologne, 23 December 1944 . . . and earned himself a posthumous VC. You may remember the very first time you operated together? It was to blitz a V1 site at Nucourt, 15 July 1944. That day, Oboe Mossies from No 105 (based at Bourn) and 109 Squadrons, together with Oboe-equipped Lancs manned by mixed 109/582 crews, led a 'box' of six heavies drawn from Nos 156, 35 and 582 Squadrons to the target. It was all hush-hush at the time but you can talk about it now. Does a snap of No 109 Squadron's 'M-Mother' throttled back to keep pace with your Lanc box help you to remember? *H. W. Lees*

119-124 Your Target Gentlemen. Every target . . . a wingbeat in the belly . . . a mixture of fear and exhilaration; each one a little more difficult . . . using up a little more of your reserve of courage . . . .

(119) Each one a bedlam of fire and smoke and haze . . . a vast, unending hotbed of pulsating brightness . . . startlingly beautiful . . . and deadly; a turmoil of gun flashes and exploding Cookies and photo flashes and burning indicators, flares and incendiaries; every one a Ruhr city or town writhing in agony. Such was the hell of 'Happy Valley'. *C. J. Woolnough*

(120) You did not always welcome nights when the weather was kind to you. As much as a night clear of cloud or haze or fog or rain helped you, so it assisted the Luftwaffe and flak regiments.

Thankfully, Saintes (a little inland from the Gironde) on the night of 23-24 June 1944 was relatively quiet. *K. Bowen-Bravery*

(121, 122) You will never know how many crews met their end due to collisions or went down under a welter of cascading bombs dropped from above. *S. W. Bridgman*

(123) A sigh of relief as you felt the 'Cookie' go with a bump, tumbling away behind the 1,000-pounders . . . heading for a city that was a city no longer . . . . *IWM*

(124) Sometimes the pictures you brought back appeared to show little more than a meaningless maze of firetracks and wavering searchlights. You suppose the intelligence boys gleaned something useful from them . . . like this one of Berlin from 15,500ft as recorded in 1943. *H. J. Davies*

119

120

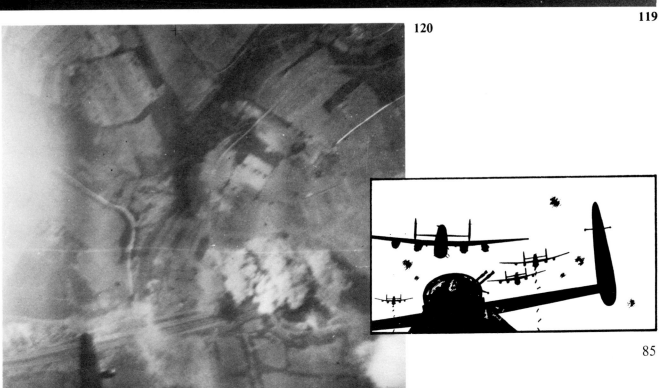

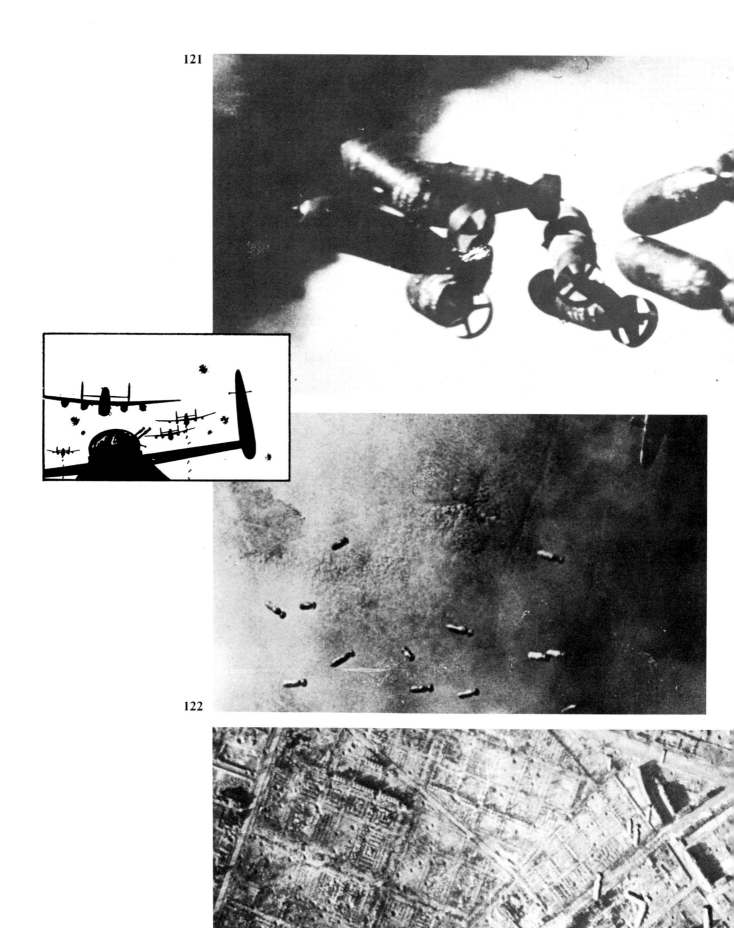

121

122

123

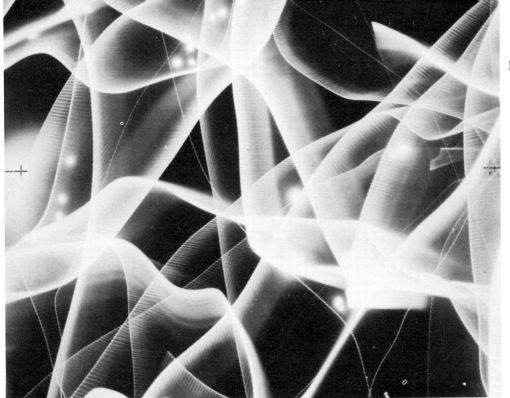

125 High-Tailing for Home. The target is behind you, fast disappearing and only visible to your mid-upper and rear gunners. It is time for the nose of your Lanc to be pushed down as you head for home. The engine note changes as your kite's throttles are pulled back, reducing the revs, and calling for re-trim accordingly. You can begin to steadily unwind, soon to relieve a bitter, salty dryness of mouth and throat when coffee flasks are opened. Coffee is like nectar after over-worked chewing gum in your mouths for the past few hours and you maybe pass round a packet of Martins Gold Leaf — strictly against the rules but you feel you have earned the right. After the tenseness even those normally quiet among you begin to chatter . . . until you are reminded of the many dangers lurking ahead. Around you are countless other Lancs, maybe Hallies too, some close in, at or near your own height, and steadily losing altitude; others preferring to stay high, firm believers in the oft preached dictum 'height means safety'. Picture is of BIII ME485 'P4:D' from No 153 Squadron, Scampton, snapped on a daylight early in 1945. (ME485 would pass to Nos 12 and 427 Squadrons before being dumped at No 10 MU, Hullavington, and declared surplus, September 1947.) *K. C. Gooch*

126

126-128 Damaging Evidence. Do you *really* hate your one-time enemy? Can you truthfully say there is any feeling of anger or loathing inside you when you deal with a German in your business affairs? Do you *really* resent the German families you meet yearly when you share a hotel or strip of beach at resorts like Nice or Alicante? Though you confess that generally you do not, do you sometimes wonder whether you hated the crews who stalked you by night, too frequently downed you, flying their 88s and 110s (that's what you called them and that's what they will always be)? You *have* mellowed. This you must accept. But you feel sure you gave the matter little thought at the age of 20. Yours was an impersonal war; you saw only an enemy intent on destroying you. And so it was you learn with those self-same night-fighter crews who fought you. Some of you have even met the men who shot you down, have become firm friends. You remember well your first meeting. They, like you, felt the tug of anxiety and apprehension ... feeling anything but confident. Yet, in no time you were swopping yarns and learning they, too, got stinko once in a while ... joined in wild mess parties ... suffered the same fears and uncertainties, elations and disappointments. The more you talked the more it seemed incredible you were once adversaries. You listened spellbound when the passing of a snapshot of your shot-up Lancaster brought forth a re-run of the night you lived to tell the tale ... discussed without bitterness the night you did *not* return ....

127

Three who made it back! (126) WO C. McLeod RCAF and crew from No 408 ('Goose') Squadron RCAF, Linton-on-Ouse were severely mauled on the night of 28-29 July 1944 when raiding Hamburg. Almost certainly pressed home from below and using upward firing guns (known as Schrage Musik), the devastating barrage from a Ju88 injured both skipper and flight engineer, in addition to badly damaging both inner Hercules engines, bomb bay and hydraulic system of BII DS730 'EQ:K'. By sheer determination the crew made it to Woodbridge emergency airfield in the small hours, where our picture was taken. Daylight and detailed study revealed such extensive damage that she never returned to squadron strength. Following partial rebuild she served out her time with conversion units until grounded (as 4973M) at Wombleton. *N. Westby*

128

(127) Mid-upper gunner Sgt D. R. Fieldhouse of No 207 Squadron had a narrow escape over Leipzig on 20-21 October 1943 when BIII ED586 'EM:F' was attacked by an unidentified night-fighter. Though machine gun and cannon fire wrecked his turret and punctured the fuselage, he was not seriously wounded; the W/op, Sgt H. O. J. Sparks was also hit and much of his equipment destroyed. To make matters worse the kite was hit by incendiaries dropped from another Lancaster flying above them, setting fire to an accumulator. Skipper Flg Off Ken Letford, by then nearing the end of his second tour, nursed his mount back to Spilsby and landed without flaps to earn himself a well-deserved DSO (he already had a DFC from his first tour on Hampdens). Both Fieldhouse and Sparks collected DFMs. ED586 survived until Stettin 5-6 January 1944. *W. C. T. Bray*

(128) It was only when you examined your kite in the cold light of day that you realised how lucky you had been. An unknown No 1 Group Lancaster bearing a night-fighter's trade mark is here inspected by ground staff. *E. D. Evans*

Stress and Strain

129, 130   Men of War. As aircrew you lived in two worlds. There was the world where one night you were hitting the high spots in town, furthering your need for friendship at 'The Trip To Jerusalem', 'The White Hart', or 'The Saracen's Head' (the so-called 'Snake Pit'), be it Nottingham, Newark, Lincoln, or elsewhere, blurring the anxieties and fears which tomorrow held amid the milling throng of kindred spirits. From there you might saunter, or stagger (dependent on how much ale you had consumed) to the local dance hall, there to pick yourself a popsy, she as eager as you for company. The next night would see you twisting and turning, fighting for your life four miles high in total blackness save for the constantly probing fingers of an endless number of searchlights; or corkscrewing to evade a fighter in a death duel as deadly as when a fly is trapped in a spider's web. Even when you returned unscathed you had experienced every known facet of human emotion. Your folks back home could never hope to understand and so on leave you talked only of episodes funny and relaxing. Even the snaps you took home (if you were lucky enough to get film that is) tended to show you in happy mood, with no hint of danger.

Here are snaps the like of which can be repeated by any crew in Bomber Command. (129) Flg Off Vic Brammar (in cockpit) and his No 7 Squadron PFF crew posing with BIII JB661 'MG:L' at Oakington, summer 1944. One of many 'above-average' crews to join PFF direct from training, they would complete their tour. (JB661 later passed to No 626 Squadron and FTR from Munich 7-8 January 1945.)   *V. Brammar*

(130) A No 150 Squadron crew (less the mid-upper gunner, who took the picture) 'chairing' their skipper, Sqn Ldr Chris Hare, at Hemswell early 1945. Their Lanc is BI ME328 'IQ:J', aptly named *Hare's Hounds*, and which outlived the war, and the squadron, before being struck off charge in November 1945. Chris Hare returned to his native Canada and his crew dispersed far and wide. Their W/op, second right, was a Free-Frenchman using the name Hay.   *J. Eyre*

129

131

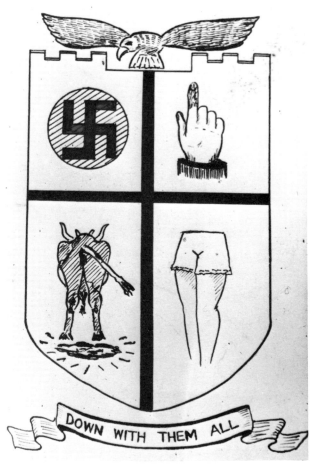

DOWN WITH THEM ALL

131, 132 Heraldry. For many of you hardly a day goes by without you recalling an incident, an individual once, like you, a member of a Lancaster crew, or maybe an airframe fitter, bowser driver — any one of a score of trades to be found on a Lancaster squadron. The recollection flashes through your mind as you go about your daily life; and it is invariably amusing for you have long since pushed the unpleasant episodes deep into the recesses of your mind. You recall the comedian in your Nissen, a Tyke who could always raise flagging spirits in times of despair; then there was the ebullient Taffy, never happier than tapping out a tune on the battered piano down at the 'Local'. The Air Force was full of such men, men of a thousand talents yet to flower to their fullest potential. Never slow to express themselves were those of you accomplished artists and cartoonists.

Here are two examples of work produced by such enterprising men. (131) How an artist from No 166 Squadron, Kirmington saw the Bombing Section in all its facets. (132) A masterful study in draughtsmanship to represent the 'Flight Engineers' Union' on No 426 ('Thunderbird') Squadron RCAF, Linton-on-Ouse. Both are self explanatory and it is hoped their publication will persuade hitherto anonymous craftsmen to come forward and identify themselves. *A. McCartney; W. McDonald*

132

426 ENGINEERS.

PER·ARDUA   AD·ELSAN

133 A Little Song Entitled. . . . Remember the parties? They were a time to forget the war for a few hours . . . to get 'smashed' and feel no pain. Tomorrow and the hard realities of a war still to be won were a world away. It was a chance to show off your latest popsy or steal someone else's; or, for those of you unattached, there were the coaches and truck loads of girls gathered in from towns and villages for miles around to charm. Conversations quickly became animated and rank meant little. Station and Squadron Commanders also let their hair down and joined in the ritual mess games. It could be some dipso' doing 'circuits and bumps' around the mess by car or motorbike, or even riding a horse! It needed little encouragement for a basic form of rugby to develop, and there was always the opportunity of leaving your footprints on the ceiling. You smile, too, at the memory of familiar faces in unfamiliar uniforms as officers wearing NCO greatcoats, battle-dresses, whatever was necessary for the occasion, were determined to join in your fun. So, too, would you NCOs be 'smuggled' into the Officers' Mess, though usually when the party was in full swing and eyes somewhat blurred. Even so, you fancy you saw more than one eye wink at you as the evening wore on! Memories to treasure.

This party is at Downham Market, home of No 635 Squadron PFF, and taking place in the Sergeants' Mess. Regaling the throng is New Zealander Wg Cdr D. W. S. Clark, presumably an invited guest. *G. D. Linacre*

133

134

134 A Rest From the War. Think back to your war and among your happiest memories will be those of improvised games of soccer or cricket on any convenient patch of grass, dirt strip, or even concrete. There is something special about the memory of a bunch of you erks challenging the aircrew to a game, often at the drop of a hat while awaiting the call for take-off; and it mattered not that you had no gear, save for a ball or a bat hurriedly mustered, nor use of a prepared pitch. It mattered little that eleven was the official complement of a team; the more the merrier was generally the rule — if rules applied! Sport was a natural ingredient of growing up for any healthy youngster, and in wartime it was an essential safety valve in lives continually under stress — too often culminating in sudden, volent death, in the case of aircrew. On a broader scale, the Service — always recreation-minded — was host to many memorable organised sporting events and among its ranks were numerous names of international repute, professional and amateur. Naturally, in this land of the game's origin every station had its soccer pitch and our snap is of a match in progress at Graveley during the season 1944/45. Centre background is No 35 ('Madras Presidency') Squadron's 'TL:M', dormant and hooded for the day, an incongruous onlooker along with the black T2 hangar beyond.
J. B. Nicholls

135 Lull and Lifeless. Be you aircrew, fitter, armourer, what-have-you, you still recall clearly countless interminable languid hours waiting for something to happen. This was seemingly a daily 'event' for those of you operating in the weeks running up to D-Day, through the long summer and into the autumn beyond. You were members of a Command under the direct control of the Allied Armies in the field and your targets could and did frequently change by the hour. It was no joke to be repeatedly briefed and later have operation after operation put back, brought forward, or cancelled altogether. Often you would be in your aircraft when the flare denoting a 'scrub' was fired . . . and the strain began to tell. Somehow you coped. If you were an armourer you, too, suffered. You ached physically and mentally and you sweated and cursed as you forever laboured changing bomb loads. You took to stacking your bombs at or near your aircraft dispersal; it broke all the rules but you had no other choice.

This view of North Killingholme (home for No 550 Squadron) could be any one of three dozen or so Lancaster aerodromes during this period. That is unless *you* were stationed there! Those of you who were, remember it as a wild and desolate 'hole' too close to the Humber Estuary in winter or periods of inclement weather.
S. B. Taylor

136, 137 Whispers. You needed relaxation. In addition to receiving seven days' leave every six weeks (which could vary depending on your squadron's fortunes), the powers-that-be fully appreciated the need to provide you with off-duty facilities.

(136) This candid snap taken in the ante-room of the Officers' Mess at North Killingholme (base for No 550 Squadron) is typical of the period. Some of its occupants can be seen catching up on the day's news while others are deep into the delights of a good book. Two play draughts or chess, while those foreground take forty winks. The carpet will be a cast-off, of uncertain origin, as will be the chairs and tables for in the austerity of wartime Britain such luxuries are in short supply. It is a far cry from the splendour to be found on prewar stations, yet, with a little ingenuity and hard work

a certain cosiness and comfort has been achieved — even if the brick wall (probably white-washed) is rather stark. Such a building — officially called a Romney but colloquially, erroneously known as a Nissen — would be found on every war emergency 'drome you served on. *K. Bowen-Bravery*

(137) A glimpse of the NCOs' recreation hall at either Binbrook or Ludford Magna. This is again a Romney, some 120ft in length, of corrugated steel-sheet construction with brick end walls and a form of composite plasterboard wall/ceiling covering. How well you remember those huge open fire grates, along with smaller black-painted stoves! At the far end can be seen a billiard/snooker table and the furniture is seen to be rather basic.
E. D. Evans

138-141 Nightmare! Does it still happen . . . a nightmare when, suddenly, the sky explodes and for one blinding moment you see every dial, every gauge in your cockpit as ahead of you a Lanc or Hally erupts in an orange ball of flame? Do you sometimes awake in your bed dripping with perspiration, sticky with sweat . . . barely conscious you are shouting . . . still twisting . . . turning . . . trying all you know to avoid a deadly volley of cannon and machine gun fire threatening to engulf you, blast you to oblivion? Are you fighting your way through a hundred arcing searchlight cones probing for prey . . . grateful for the chance to slip through unnoticed when they lock on to some poor sods you can see getting clobbered . . . knowing they would do the same were it you out there squirming and diving . . . knowing it might be you in trouble tomorrow night, whenever. Are you amid fighter flares cascading above and ahead of you in a blaze of yellow light, soon to envelop you in sulphurous mist, exposing you to every fighter within miles?

Do you relive Stuttgart or Magdeburg or Duisburg . . . any of two dozen cauldrons of flame and smoke and death spread out beneath you like some gigantic magic garden . . . the yellow blossoming flashes of Cookies mingling with green markers and lines of glowing white incendiaries, flowering red as they gain a hold and spread to form a vivid, deadly riot of colour . . . so bright its glare fills your cockpit, your turret with an eerie, sinister glow.

(138) Are you in for a nightmare, through eyeing a scarecrow and flak puffs over the Ruhr in 1942? (No-one will ever convince you there were no such things as scarecrows!). Would you rather see Calais under attack in daylight (139) as shot on film from a No 463 Squadron RAAF Lancaster in 1944 . . . or (140, 141) No 617 Squadron's BI (Special) Lancs blasting the bridge at Nienburg, 22 March 1945 with Grand Slams.
British Official; W. H. Hodge; British Official (2)

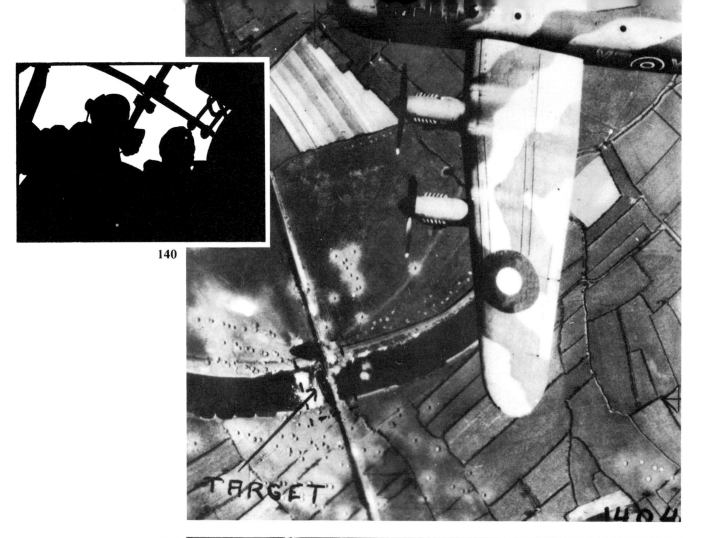

140

141

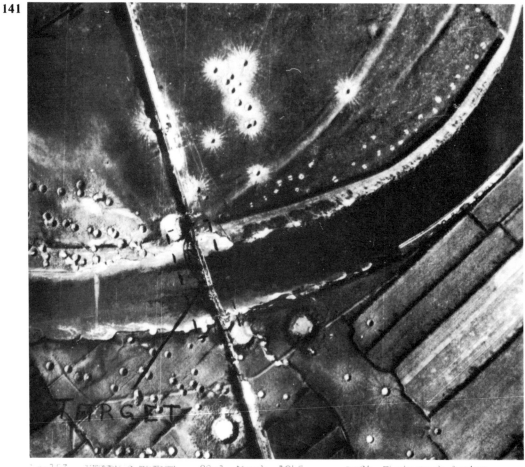

No. 195. NIENBURG BRIDGE. 22nd. March, 1945. — Left: Photograph during attack. Right: Subsequent reconnaissance photograph shows the complete destruction of the bridge, together with the greater part of the approach viaducts. (5 GROUP)

CONFIDENTIAL

H.Q.B.C. AIR STAFF INT. P.I.   G.-628

Superstition and Custom

142 Get Some In! As far as you were concerned, *your* squadron was the best in Bomber Command. It could out-fly, out-fight, out-drink and out-fun any outfit you cared to mention. Come to think of it, when it came to seducing and laying the women, your squadron was the best at that too! Mind you, as you read the odd letter from a pal serving with a Canadian or Australian squadron, and he described the sumptuous food parcels his crew received from home, you did sometimes wish you were elsewhere! Being with a Canadian squadron in 6 Group had decided advantages if you liked good living. Take No 431 ('Iroquois') Squadron RCAF at Croft as being typical. They were 'adopted' by Simcoe in Ontario and its townsfolk regularly sent home-comforts in many forms to the unit's air and ground crews. The town even sent the squadron a mascot, nicknamed 'Minnie Simcoe' here seen posing for her picture with CO Wg Cdr Eric Mitchell RCAF in the cockpit of an Iroquois Lanc X, 13 November 1944. Minnie is reputed to have completed a full tour of operations yet, unaccountably, no-one seems to remember what became of her when 431 returned to Canada in June 1945. Any idea? *Public Archives of Canada*

143, 144   A Breed Apart. Superstitions among you abounded. No different to most of us — who does not touch wood, walk round a ladder rather than under it, or carry a St Christopher's medallion? — you aircrew of the day knew no bounds when it came to the carrying of mascots and good luck charms, or performing 'rituals' before taking to the air against the enemy. Even those of you who frowned on such practices found yourselves uneasy should one of your crew attempt to take off without a certain scarf sent by a devoted mother, a silk stocking or an item of underwear from a girl friend, a rabbit's foot given by an aunt. Had there been observers of human nature roving the bomber airfields before a trip they would have filled several note books recording the variety of articles, and the breed of men carrying them: as a robust soccer-playing gunner you were just as likely to stuff a rag doll in your tunic as would a studious chess-loving navigator! Then there were the weird and wonderful customs performed by you as individuals or complete crews. For *your* crew it may be simply urinating against the tail wheel, or entering the kite in a set order — often practices dating back to OTU days; or perhaps you would all line up to rub or tap a stuffed rabbit or gollywog hung inside the Lanc's rear door or suspended from the cockpit roof. Equally, some of you went to war wearing such diverse apparel as cowboy boots, a top hat, or carrying a brolly, even a lavatory brush; and on some stations whole squadrons would observe sacred rituals: a record of 'The Shrine of St Cecilia' always played in the Sergeants' Mess at No 50 Squadron, Skellingthorpe is a typical example.

Here (143) No 9 Squadron rear gunner Flt Sgt 'Pinky' Hayler and his wireless operator, Flt Sgt 'Cheeky' Lever present an outwardly happy study as they show off their respective mascots, Lever also gripping a cane always carried by his skipper, Sqn Ldr Dickie Bunker, OC 'B' Flight. The picture was taken at Bardney before one of the series of four Hamburg fire storm raids begun on the night of 24-25 July 1943 and ending 2-3 August. The Bunker crew completed their tour.   *R. G. Lomas*

(144) Sgt Danny Driscoll spitting on the tail fin of No 150 Squadron's BI NG264 'IQ:B', named 'We Dood It Too' (regular mount of Flg Off Gordon Markes and crew) at Hemswell circa March 1945 and representative of an exhaustive list of 'customs' staged by aircrew. (The Markes' septet would leave Hemswell an emeritus crew; NG264 would be flown to No 10 MU, Hullavington, May 1946 and be broken up 10 months later.) *L. G. Buckell*

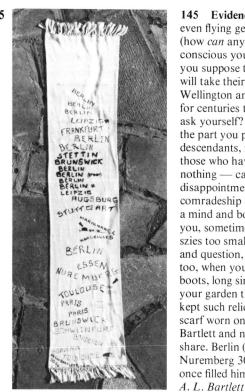

145   Evidence in Silk. Whenever you hear of log books, medals, even flying gear changing hands for, to you, lewd sums of money (how *can* any man's life be measured in terms of money?), you are conscious you belong to history. Just as with all the wars before, you suppose that Bomber Command's years of trial and endeavour will take their place alongside the campaigns of Cromwell and Wellington and become study for debate by historians and pundits for centuries to come. What will they make of it all, you sometimes ask yourself? Long after you are gone the few tangible reminders of the part you played in the Hitler war will fail to tell your descendants, museums, researchers what you went through. Only those who have been in battle can know this. No book, no film — nothing — can recapture the agonies and fears, the disappointments and elations; nor, too, the privations, the comradeship . . . any and every sense and emotion it is possible for a mind and body to endure, sustain. As the mood or occasion takes you, sometimes you muse over a fading battledress (now several szies too small), a silk scarf, buried deep in a trunk in your attic . . . and question, no matter how fleetingly, that it happened at all! So, too, when you clear out your shed and come across your flying boots, long since abandoned following more mileage done digging your garden than when flying all those years ago. Few of you have kept such relics in the pristine condition here evident with this silk scarf worn on every trip by No 50 Squadron bomb aimer Les Bartlett and now presented to the RAF Museum for the nation to share. Berlin (10 times) . . . Leipzig 19-20 February 1944 . . . Nuremberg 30-31 March 1944 . . . these and other names which once filled him with dread, sewn into the silk for posterity. *A. L. Bartlett*

Trial and Terror

146 By Now it was Routine. Thirty times or more you began the day by learning you were on the battle order. Thirty times or more you meandered down to the flights, in twos and threes, on your bikes (or someone else's!), the crisp morning air-slowly instilling life into weary bodies and bleary eyes following a boozy night in town. Already the erks were there, well into their DIs, and you kicked your heels awhile until you could begin your own checks and wring out any wrinkles on an air test. In no time at all you were there again, now wide awake and on the brink of a great adventure, an enterprise you will never forget for the rest of your life. Your first trip . . . what memories that holds. You were excited yet fearful; keen yet uncertain; wanting to go yet inwardly hoping for a scrub. It was the beginning of a love-hate relationship: love for the unique spirit of aircrew and squadron life, and for an aircraft without peer; hate for the job you had to do. Before that first trip you were rather too talkative, eager to pick up tit-bits of gen, talking about anything to take your mind off what lay ahead. You came back somehow

different, more subdued; you had crossed the barrier between life and death and returned, and you felt mentally aged — all within the space of a few hours. You would feel like old men before you were through.

A flood of memories must crowd the minds of you one-time warriors eyeing Canadian Flg Off Lloyd Freidman and his No 405 ('Vancouver') Squadron RCAF crew here preparing for a flight at Gransden Lodge on a November day heavy with a leaden sky. An engine fitter still works on the port-outer of BIII PA982 'LQ:E' newly 'acquired' by the Friedman crew, already veterans of over 30 ops (20 with main force on Hallies) and having recently graduated to the role of primary blind marker. They would complete an outstanding double tour by taking PA982 to Mannheim in daylight, 1 March 1945, their 24th in her since Homberg, 25 October 1944, again a daylight. (PA982 would survive the conflict and end her days of usefulness as an ASR/GRIII until wrecked in May 1947). Few dispersals could boast a bike rack! *S. D. Smith*

While Other Mortals Sleep

Behind us lies the land we know,
Before, the hostile sea,
Thank God that man can not foretell
Calamities to be.

Beneath our wings he slumbers on,
The unsuspecting foe;
He does not heed us as we come,
Lord help us when we go!

Astern we leave the flames of Hell,
The North Sea lies ahead,
A battered kite, a tired crew,
O' for base and bed!

English soil,
But don't relax,
Remember Sergeant Brown,
Almost on the runway
When intruders shot him down.

Philip A. Nicholson

146

147, 148 With a Grinding of Gears You were Gone. By the time
you heard the familiar squeal of brakes outside the locker rooms to
herald arrival of the crew buses, much of the lively banter between
yours and some twenty plus crews had by then largely subsided.
What talking and joking there still was tended to come from the
new crews. It was always the same. Too soon they would enter with
a shock another world, from which they would return silent and
brooding. After five ops — if they survived that long — they would
be old hands. The build-up of tension which had steadily mounted
ever since seeing your crew's names on the battle order in the
morning, now approached fever pitch as you stepped outside and
prepared to board. It was not so bad while you kept yourself busy
handing in your valuables, collecting your 'chutes and escape kits,
sorting your sandwiches and coffee flasks, taking your time
climbing into your gear . . . but once inside that infernal truck your
stomach really began to churn and flutter. That bumpy ride around
the peri-track was for all the world like sitting in a waiting room,
awaiting your fate in the dentist's chair. . . .

Two years separate the scenes shown. (147) No 106 Squadron
crews about to board the crew bus at Syerston, winter 1942/43,
fully togged out with all the operational gear of the day, including
Mae Wests, fur-lined flying boots, and bright yellow Taylor suits
(gunners only and an example visible far left). (148) Mildenhall,
May 1945, before an 'Exodus' trip and noteworthy for a number of
pointers clearly dating the picture. The aircrew (No 15 Squadron)
wear their 'every day' walking boots, not flying boots.
J. F. Wickins, D. A. Russell

14

148

Soon the Take-off, Soon the War

We bustle urgently between dispersals;
One by one the aircrews disembark
And slouch with studied negligence
To waiting Lancs, monstrous in the growing dark.
We, the last to go, mutter our farewells,
Stretch our legs in new-made space, and trundle on
To our more distant rendezvous;
Our eagerness to be away and gone
Diminished by awareness that not all of us
Who scramble noisily aboard to-night
Will share the thankful journey back
From darkness into light.

Philip A. Nicholson

149, 150 Chill of Cold Suspense. You recall the agony of apprehension you felt before your first trip. You experienced a feeling in your gut such as you had back at school before an examination, or awaiting your fate when standing outside the headmaster's study. As you lay on your bed, or wherever you tried to relax, you were feeling decidedly scared. Your stomach really began to tighten up . . . your mouth was dry . . . you were beginning to feel clammy. You were each silent with your thoughts and you tried desperately to appear calm. A thousand thoughts filled your head: would you let your crew down? . . . could you cope? Finally the silence was broken when one of you plucked up courage to ask the others how they felt. You were relieved when all your crew admitted they, too, were 'scared bloody stiff'. As the time drew near an impatience to get started surmounted your nervousness. Approaching the briefing room one part of you longed to break into

a run, the other restrained you; no matter how quickly you got there you had still to wait. You tried to convince yourself that new crews were always blooded on 'easy' targets, one of many rumours with you since training school; one glance at your navigator's map made you think otherwise, though none of you yet knew the actual target. By the time the transport arrived to take you to the kites you were talking a lot, lighting up one cigarette after another as though they were going out of fashion, walking up and down . . . raring to go . . .

(149) A Binbrook full of noise and action stages a No 460 Squadron RAAF crew making final preparations in their dispersal near the runway's end, while behind them the first Lanc gets under way (circa December 1943). (150) Resigned to taking on Berlin yet again, No 61 Squadron crews experience the inevitable wait for transport at Syerston, winter 1943/4.   *F. E. Harper; H. N. Scott*

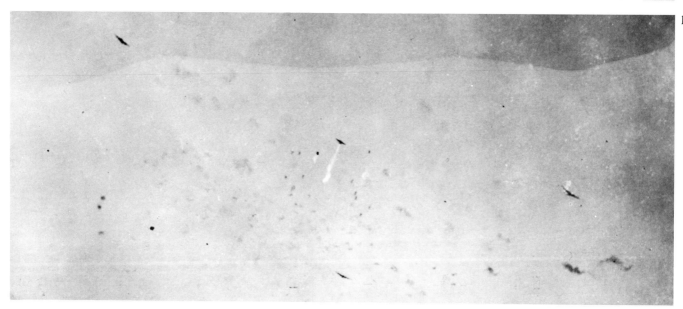

15

151, 152 Deadly Encounters. Remember your first daylight . . . your first clear view of flak? You were serenely approaching the target, drawing comfort from the fellow Lancs around you, and fighter umbrella high above, when you saw your first daylight flak barrage. Suddenly, in front of the stream the sky was pimpled with a wall of flak punching upwards. Something twisted inside your stomach and you thought how impossible it was to fly through that barrage and emerge unscathed. You went on . . . not wanting to . . . wanting to do anything else but go on . . . but going on just the same. Then the tight rolling balls of jet black smoke began drifting through the gaggle towards you, thinning out and changing shape as they came. You could actually see the flash and flame in the bursts and you wondered whether a gun crew down below had you in their sights. You felt alone in the sky . . . then, with the target unfolding beneath you, there was no more time for thought. You had, of course, experienced flak while flying at night . . . had felt your kite shudder and bounce due to a near burst sending slivers of deadly shrapnel in all directions, each a hammer blow on the thin, less than one quarter-inch-thick skin that was your fuselage and wings; it was usually too late, but fatal, if you could see or smell it!

Here two dramatic panoramas of the sky over Dusseldorf, Christmas Eve 1944, as snapped by Canadian wireless operator Flg Off Neil Taschuk from the astrodome of a No 434 ('Bluenose') Squadron RCAF Lanc X (skipper: Flt Lt Warrie Rothenbush RCAF). In one picture a kite is seen to be hit and trailing smoke, soon to wheel away from the stream before plummeting earthwards to burn on alien soil. *Both N. G. Taschuk*

153 Jump or Roast. Fire, whether in the air or on the ground was an omnipresent threat. When it happened you had to suppress your sheer inner terror and desire to get away regardless of the consequences; cool-headed self discipline was your only salvation. You well knew your Lancaster was little more than an airborne bomb carrier and fuel tank; and you knew, too, how volatile petrol was — also fumes — and did not need reminding that a wing fire could mean you had but two minutes before the main spar burned through. You repaid all those who had repeatedly stressed the need for continual practice on how to deal with such an emergency, by mentally and physically preparing yourself for when the time came. The inner panic you momentarily felt was quickly stifled and you found yourself co-ordinating mind and body with quite remarkable automation.

Here No 44 (Rhodesia) Squadron's BI R5494 'KM:O' well alight at North Front, Gibraltar, 7 July 1942. Plt Off J. D. V. S. Stephens and crew had flown to Gib' to pick up Plt Off D. F. Nicholson and crew, also from 44 and who had ditched their Lanc in mid-Atlantic on 14 June while on convoy duty during the squadron's partial secondment to Coastal Command. When landing, R5494 hit a fragment of AA shrapnel lying on the runway, burst a tyre, and slithered to a spectacular halt, with fire imminent. All aboard were out in no time and, minus two precious Lancs, both crews returned to home base Waddington. Regrettably neither crew survived their tours; the Nicholson seven did not return from Frankfurt, 24-25 August 1942, whilst Stephens and company went down on Wismar 1-2 October of the same year. *K. P. Smales*

153

154 With Your Own Eyes. About to pancake at a soaking Binbrook is No 460 Squadron's 'AR:P', snapped by some enterprising bod braving the elements and whose camera lens records the lashing rain. Following a tiring flight you will have called up Flying Control when still some way out — maybe even 'telling a fib' about your true position for it is not unknown for a crew to give a false height and heading and thus avoid the bind of stacking above or close to the aerodrome. Letting down through the swirling cloud banks is a far from pleasant experience and seven pairs of bleary eyes stand out like stalks peering through the rain squalls for a glimpse of the ground and first the outer, then inner marker. Even with the aid of SBA your final touch-down will be visual and with rain hitting the windscreen at over 100mph the wipers and de-icers simply cannot cope. Up front you are forced to open the small triangular-shaped direct-vision panels of the cockpit, thrusting your heads almost into the biting gale force airflow, one eye focused obliquely ahead. Suddenly, as if miraculously, there are the lights and in no time you are rounding out and lining up, soon to identify the pundit. Seconds away now and despite the beating rain there is the runway, like some endless great belt stretching ahead, awash and shiny black. . . . *B. Addyman*

155

155 Frozen Smiles. Each time you crossed the bleak expanse that was the North Sea ('The Oggin'), always the thought was with you that you might one day, or night, be giving it a close inspection. The prospect was far from inviting. When the prospect turned to a distinct probability, you had ahead of you a less than even chance of being spotted by your own or the enemy's rescue services. More likely you would meet an untimely end due to drowning or exposure. It was one thing to nurse your kite above the heaving swell in daylight, but at night the same experience was a journey into the unknown. You looked out into the infinite blackness — so recently comforting, shielding you from your foe — and you well knew that even if you survived the ensuing ditching, the icy waters could claim your life long before morning and a rescue craft could find you. So, you sat in the darkness, all of you, each alone with your thoughts . . . and waited. You had jettisoned every removable piece of equipment in order to eke out the fuel, but you listened anxiously as your engineer called out the fuel state. You dreaded the panel lights winking red, first one, then all in a row, and you mentally went through your ditching drill over and over again, so often practised in the hangar back at base, a bore, second nature to you, but which now just might save your life. When the time came to land on the water you needed a good measure of skill and composure. Judging the swell and attendant spray brought out the best in a pilot and was an added trial of strength and nerve. You well knew that a Lancaster was not the best of aircraft to ditch; they were prone to break their backs and you had precious few seconds to act once your kite settled on to the water. This is typical of a winter ditching, said to be dated 20 December 1943, a chilling picture taken by an Air-Sea Rescue aircraft of Coastal Command. Some of the Lanc's crew huddle together in one dinghy, while they tow another which is significantly empty. . . . *S. T. Andrews*

156, 157   So This is How We Thank Her For Bringing Us Home.
Limping home on a 'wing and a prayer', shot to hell by flak or
fighters, one or more engines dead, one or more of your crew dead
or comatose, was when courage shone through like a bright star.
That and tenacity which saw you through a turbulent, pulsing night
of torment; a night when you faced nerve-rending miles over a
North Sea below in the inky void, unrelenting, bitter waters getting
uncomfortably closer as your remaining motors strained to keep
you airborne and you heaved overboard anything and everything
you could prise loose with the axe, your bare hands. Each of you
began to feel recurring waves of fatigue sweeping over you . . .
could feel yourself falling, spinning each time you momentarily
closed your aching eyes, their lids so heavy you visibly winced. You
tried desperately to keep your mind active — anything but dwell on
the fearful prospect ahead, below . . . all the time staring into the
darkness, knowing you were alone, hoping you passed unnoticed.
Nothing could hasten the second hand which jerked its way —
never faster, never slower — round the luminous dial of your
watch. Nothing could shorten the miles of alien blackness

stretching before you. Nothing could hasten the welcome glow of
goose-necks at Carnaby or Woodbridge or Manston. . . .

This is the wreck of No 626 Squadron's BIII PB961 'UM:X²'
recorded by the ever busy Manston photographer, 3 January 1945.
Flg Off WAT White RCAF and crew — engineer and rear gunner
injured by cannon fire splinters — just failed to make it at Manston
emergency 'drome on return from Osterfeld, 31 December 1944.
'Chalky' White and crew recovered quickly from their ordeal and
left Wickenby and the war in one piece; PB961 was dismantled and
junked.   *Both J. H. N. Molesworth*

158, 159 Minus One for the Tigers. Prangs! How many of you can say you never experienced the indignity of splaying your undercart beneath you as your instructor and fellow pupils stood and watched . . . or descended with alarming rapidity to greet the whitecaps of an angry Irish Sea when one motor of the Botha carting you and other gunners on a stooge from Mona or Castle Kennedy, decided to quit. Statistically, as six individuals mastering your trade at schools for gunners, bomb aimers and navs, engineers, drivers and w/ops, you stood every chance of having some time 'come downstairs' in a hurry. Even should you have come through your early months of learning free of incident, there is the probability that collectively your crew of seven bent the odd Wellington or Whitley, Halifax or Stirling when working your way through OTU, HCU. No? Not even a runaway prop, or bellying in when all of you unaccountably failed to hear the Klaxon telling you the undercart had not been selected? Remarkable! Whatever, whenever, wherever was your 'hairy do', one or more, when on the treadmill that led up to your squadron, it was as nothing compared with the real test when it came. And those tests of nerve and stamina were there for you to endure, sustain, right up to the time the lights of Europe came on again. And you get angry when you read that ops were supposedly a doddle in 1945. True, they could not be compared with the Ruhr and Berlin bashings of 1943/4; yet, too many guys would argue the point could they speak from the grave.

Such a test of nerve and stamina faced Plt Off Rob McInroy RCAF and crew of No 424 ('Tiger') Squadron RCAF on return from Zweibrucken on the night of 14-15 March 1945. When in the Skipton circuit, BI NN777's controls suddenly refused to respond. No amount of effort could free them and in no time at all the Lanc entered into a left-hand downward spiral. Somehow they made it to Dishforth and bellied in by the dim glow of goose-necks at 23.45hrs. In the photos taken on 20 March, NN777 'QB:F' had been dragged to the hangars for salvage (for some reason lacking her dorsal turret fairing). Minus one for the Tigers.
Both T. Waddington Collection

There is no Accounting for Fate

Stan Bridgman and Frank Bone

Well into the month of February 1945, crews could be entitled to expect things to be getting easier. The Allies were well on top in the land battles on the Continent, and the Luftwaffe, despite record production of aircraft, felt the great loss of experienced pilots sustained in Operation 'Baseplate', and — more significantly — the great shortage of fuel, so acute, that only the top line pilots were allowed combat flying time (the fuel shortage due to No 5 Group's hammering of refineries and the transport system). However, the Luftwaffe continued to fight with great tenacity as did the ground anti-aircraft defences both by day and night.

By this stage of the war, many Lancaster aircrews, particularly in No 3 Group based in the southern sector of East Anglia, and the Canadians of No 6 Group in Yorkshire and Durham were engaged almost wholly on daylight operations, some crews completing a tour of ops in only three months (a tour could be 35, or even 40 ops by now), such was the intensity of the sorties. Yet some squadrons, mainly in 'Cocky's Air Force' (5 Group) were still pounding away almost exlusively by night virtually to the bitter end. There was no escape from retribution in the final months of the war.

On the night of 21 February 1945 for instance, a large force of 'heavies' was despatched including Lancasters from No 463 Squadron RAAF, Waddington whose target was the Mittleland-Ems Canal (near Gravenhorst) which was still in use as a main artery for the transport of supplies to the German army. Bomber Command was a regular visitor to this target and the Dortmund-Ems Canal, for as soon as the reconnaissance aircraft reported that these canals had been repaired, the bombers would strike again. The Germans had extracted a high cost in aircraft and crews, and in February 1945, because of the chaotic state of the rail and road system, the value of these strategic waterways demanded extreme vigilance from the night-fighters of the Luftwaffe. On No 463 Squadron's battle order for the raid was Lancaster B1 NG329, 'JO-Z' *Zebra*, to be manned by Flg Off Graham H. Farrow, RAAF, and crew, which comprised: B/A, WO Russel Bermingham RAAF; F/E, Sgt Stan Bridgman RAF; Nav, Flg Off Pete Harris RAF; W/Op, Flt Sgt Jack Wiltshire, RAAF; M/U, Sgt Frank Bone RAF; R/G, Sgt Stan Clay RAF.

This was to be the 15th time they had set out together for enemy-held territory since joining No 463 Squadron in November 1944 via 1661 Heavy Conversion Unit, Winthorpe, and No 5 Lancaster Finishing School, Syerston. They had suffered two frustrating 'aborts' (one recall and one boomerang) but had successfully completed 12 attacks, all but two at night, which had included such distant targets as Munich, Gdynia and Politz involving round trips of over 10 hours. The majority of these operations had been done in Lancaster B1 LM130 — with gaudy *Nick the Nazi Neutralizer* motif emblazoned on her nose (officially 'N-Nan', but to the ground and aircrews 'Old Nick'). On this particular night, however, Nick was in the hangar for a major inspection and service after completing 86 operational sorties

— a 'major' being a fairly rare luxury for a Lanc, even at this late stage of the conflict.

The story of the fateful night is taken up by the mid-upper gunner, Frank Bone, who wrote this account only two weeks after the event:

'Take-off time was 17.07hrs and we were flying "JO-Z" as "N-Nan" was in the hangar on a major inspection. The bomb load was 14×1,000-pounders. Petrol load was 1,600 plus 50gal. H-hour was to be 20.30.

'It was quite a pleasant trip out and we bombed dead on time, 20.34 as we were in the last wave. After leaving the target the flak seemed to die down, but apparently the fighters were on the job. I counted seven kites going down in flames, so we knew there were fighters around, as by this time there was no flak at all. Stan, the rear gunner and I were reporting these to Pete the navigator so that he could log them. We

were worried because we still had a 1,000lb bomb "hung up" in the bomb bay. After Russ checked we were still over enemy occupied territory, he decided to see if we could get rid of the b.... thing, otherwise we would have to keep it until we were over the Channel.

'Graham, the skipper, put the aircraft in level flight and the bomb doors were opened. It was a great relief to all of us when we heard Russ's voice over the I/C say "Bomb gone". We resumed our banking searches once again when suddenly we were hit in the starboard-inner engine from below. Cannon shells flashed past Jack, the wireless operator and also shattered the navigator's table. They seemed to come at an angle of about 60-80 degrees with the floor and from the starboard quarter down.

'Graham gave the order "Put on parachutes", also telling Lofty, the engineer, to feather the starboard-inner engine, as

160

160 The Hunters. Major Heinz-Wolfgang Schnaüfer ('The Ghost of St Trond') and crew — the only complete night-fighter team to win Knight's Crosses. Gunner Wilhelm Gänsler is on his right; radar operator Fritz Rümpelhardt stands on his left.
F. Rümpelhardt

161 The Hunted. On diversion to Ford following a daylight to the Urft Dam, 8 December 1944 — their second op, Flg Off Graham Farrow RAAF and crew pause for a snapshot. Left to right: flight engineer, Flt Sgt Stan Bridgman; bomb aimer, WO Russ Bermingham RAAF; wireless operator, Flt Sgt Jack Wiltshire RAAF; navigator, Flg Off Pete Harris; pilot, Flg Off Graham Farrow RAAF; mid-upper gunner, Sgt Frank Bone; rear gunner, Sgt Stan Clay. *S. W. Bridgman*

it was, by this time, on fire. A couple of seconds later the skipper gave the order to jump as the whole wing was ablaze and the engines would not feather. (The accumulator had been hit.) The lights were going off and on, mainly off. I came out of my turret and sat on the step to put on my parachute. By this time, Stan the rear gunner had opened the rear door. I moved back towards the rear of the kite and stood on the step of the doorway. I could see the wing burning and before I knew what was happening, Stan pushed me, and out I went. (I had hold of my ripcord all the time.) I just glimpsed the tailplane rushing past and the next thing I knew, I was dangling in midair. I don't even remember pulling my ripcord. I looked up to see if my 'chute had opened as I didn't seem to be moving at all. I felt as if I was hanging in space. To my relief it was open, and I was just sailing smoothly down when I saw what appeared to be an Me109 fly past me at about 200 yards distance. I thought, "This is it" as I expected him to come in and have a crack at me. Luckily he flew right past me and headed in the direction of Germany.

'I was still a good way off the ground and could see our kite plunging earthwards in a ball of flame. Another was hit a little later and that met the same fate as our own, and the other seven before us. By this time I could see the "deck" quite clearly, and the roadways and haystacks in my vision were getting rapidly bigger. I had no sooner prepared myself for the impact when I landed and fell backwards. Surprisingly I didn't hurt myself at all.

'As I did not know where I had landed I released my parachute and was going to get rid of it when I saw two chaps coming towards me, as I had landed right by a lane. One came out of a farmhouse on the opposite side of the road and the other was running down the lane. I thought my time

162, 163 For Nick Read Zebra.
(162) With her nose turret turned fully to port, B1 LM130 'JO:N' looks positively sinister and menacing at Waddington, winter 1944/5. (163) B1 NG329 'JO:Z' in happier times. Another No 463 Squadron RAAF crew (engineer Sgt Sid Shorthouse standing back to camera) on hand to load 'Window' at Waddington, early 1945.
RAAF Official

was up so all I could do was raise my hands and be taken prisoner. I was overjoyed when I heard one of them say: "Tommy, Tommy, dis is Ollande". They picked my 'chute up (they were after the silk) and took me to a farmhouse across the lane. I tried to explain that I wanted to get in touch with the Army authorities; I think they understood because they took me up the lane to another house, a big one. There, to my surprise, I found Russ. Boy, was I glad to see him! I put my arms round him and hugged him. The Dutch folk made us a cup of tea and gave us a cigarette, and did I enjoy it! Meanwhile, they had phoned through to Army headquarters and so a truck was sent for us. It was great to see and hear someone who could speak English again.

'The driver took us a little way along a road where we were overjoyed to find Pete who told us that the rest of the crew were in a farmhouse farther along and had all landed safely, but Lofty was wounded in both legs from fragments of cannon shell fired by the fighter. Lofty had had his trouser leg ripped off and was all bandaged up when we arrived. Still, we were all safe and alive, thank God.

'Pete told us we jumped 21.11hrs which was just over half an hour after leaving the target, and our height was 6,000ft. We landed four miles inside our lines, so it's a good job we didn't get it a couple of minutes earlier, or else!!! Graham had lost one of his boots while descending, so he borrowed one of Lofty's. I lost the torch which I carried in my flying boot, but why worry, I could get another when I got back.'

Thanks to training disciplines and the courage of the pilot Graham Farrow, the entire crew survived. Only after first ensuring his crew had gone did he leave his seat. By the time he reached the escape hatch in the nose, the Lancaster had become inverted in her death plunge, and he had to climb up out of the hatch instead of merely dropping through, and was snatched clear by the slipstream, which had also released his parachute only seconds before 'JO-Z' hit the ground.

The only casualty was the flight engineer, Stan Bridgman, who recalls the events quite clearly:
'I had left my seat to check the engineer's panel, and was standing in front of it when the first and only burst of fire caused this panel literally to disappear. I felt two vicious punches in my legs, and fell over. On the pilot's instruction I endeavoured to feather the starboard engines, but the night-fighter's cannon shells had done their work, and it was not possible to do so. By this time both engines were on fire, and the pilot had started his fight to keep the aircraft level to enable his crew to obey his next order which was "JUMP! JUMP!"

'It was at this moment the bomb aimer questioned the order by asking "Did you say 'JUMP'?", and I remember thinking: 'This is a hell of a time to hold a debate'. However, the inrush of air from the opened hatch told me that No 1 had gone. As No 2 to exit I dragged myself to the bomb aimer's compartment, and then realised my chest-'chute was still in its stowage so I went back for it. Having obtained this somewhat necessary piece of equipment I looked through the hatch into the night; my next thought was to put my head through it and as I did so the slipsteam hit me and I made my exit in classic style, just as all the instructors had said we

should — a head first somersault. I counted the "10' in very quick time and pulled on the ring, extending my left arm to its full extent then letting the ring drop. A hard jerk told me my 'chute had opened, and with the speed of my fall arrested, I became aware of our Lanc, poor old "Z-Zebra", a blaze of fire from the starboard wing, heading away; and then the sound of the wind in the parachute cords was the best music I have ever heard. I did not see "JO-Z" crash. It was very dark, and I kept loose limbed, and hit the ground quite reasonably.

'I could hear a dog barking near by, and due to the speed of events had no idea where I was, Holland or Germany. I gathered my 'chute, and started to push it into the nearby hedgerow. I heard movement nearby and a voice shouted "There's one" in English. I shouted back: "Are you a Limey?", and then out of the dark appeared two soldiers wearing the renowned "Red Beret", part of a parachute division holding the line. I was unable to walk, so the soldiers carried me to a nearby farm and into the barn where the Dutch family Van Lipzig were forced to live due to their farmhouse having been destroyed by shell fire.

'First aid was given to me, and in the next few minutes other members of the crew were brought in. Transport arrived, and the Army lads took me to an advance aid post for further medical attention. After this I was taken to Helmond in Holland where a school had been converted to an army hospital. The following morning I was operated on for the removal of cannon shell splinters and attention to the damage done by the bullets which had passed through my thighs. It was painful, but when I thought that had the aircraft been three feet lower I probably would have been dead. I counted my blessings.'

There seems little doubt that Farrow and crew were the victims of the guns of the Me110 piloted by the CO of Nachtjagdgeschwader No 4, Major Heinz-Wolfgang Schnaüfer, at 23-years-old the undoubted 'Ace of Aces' among the Luftwaffe's night-fighter pilots, with film star looks to match his undoubted ability. Known as 'The Ghost of St Trond' (the unit's base in Belgium) he had flown Me110s since June 1942. His crew consisted of Fritz Rümpelhardt (radar operator) who had joined Schnaüfer when his total was 21 victories, and Wilhelm Gänsler (gunner) who had been with Schnaüfer from the start.

On this particular night the fighters were to score heavily. The ground radar stations responsible for initial guidance to the vicinity of the bombers did their job well, as did the airborne radar operators to whom fell the task of final location of individual targets. The path of the returning bomber stream was clearly marked by the pyres of numerous downed victims. NJG 4 was operating from Gutersloh (ironically now an RAF base), and in the space of two minutes, between 20.43 and 21.03hrs, Schnaüfer and crew, using their upward-firing guns, 'Schrage Muzik', shot down seven four-engined bombers, all logged as Lancasters. On their eighth attack from below another Lancaster, the guns of their Me110 jammed after a short burst, and though hits were seen to be made, the attack had to be broken off without the night-fighter crew seeing any end result. If it was, in fact, 'JO-Z',

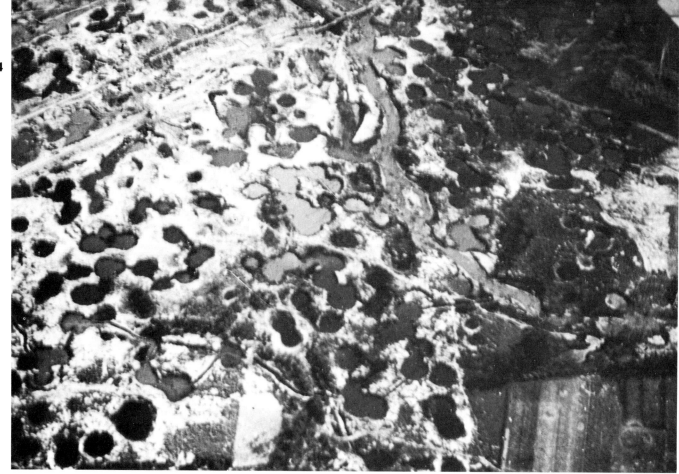

they had hit and mortally wounded the Lanc, but the jamming of the guns possibly spared the lives of the aircrew who baled out at 21.11 one minute after the Me110's final combat that night which is logged by Fritz Rümpelhardt as 21.10, with altitude and course coinciding; and the Lancaster did receive only a single short burst of fire.

As it was, on that black night, four night-fighter crews alone accounted for 28 of the 62 bombers lost out of 800 despatched. No 463 Squadron lost two others, both returning from the Mitteland raid; one (PB804, 'JO-A') was flown by its CO, Wg Cdr W. A. Forbes DSO, DFC, who was well into his second tour of ops, and a fine leader of men.

What became of the leading actors in this night of drama?

Graham Farrow and crew (minus their injured engineer) were picked up from Eindhoven by a specially despatched No 463 Squadron Lanc only three days after their bale-out, and were operating again with their squadron very soon after their return, with a replacement engineer, going on to complete 23 ops before peace came.

Stan Bridgman, after a spell in the RAF Hospital at Wroughton, rejoined his old crew mates for a final fling in late May '45, ten days' flying on Operation 'Wastage', the disposal of surplus incendiaries in the North Sea, together again in 'JO-N' but not their old 'Nick'.

LM130 had emerged from her 'major' and was allocated to a new crew, only to collide with a Hurricane on a fighter affiliation exercise, crashing with the loss of all aboard near Metheringham on 11 March 1945.

Graham Farrow and his former crew members all survive, and are still in contact 35 years after the events described. In 1980 the W/Op and F/eng went back to Venray and visited the Van Lipzig family who assisted them after their

164 Missed! The Farrow crew take another look at the Mitteland Canal — this time while on a Cook's Tour, May 1945. A snap taken by Aussie W/op Jack Wiltshire. *S. W. Bridgman*

unexpected arrival at the farm. They visited, too, the woods at Ysselsten, where the remains of 'JO-Z' still rest, including a portion of fuselage with its row of Tucker rivets looking as though they had only just left the factory. Such was the quality of the Lancaster.

They have also met Fritz Rümpelhardt, who is an administrative officer at an agricultural college in West Germany. They learned that after the war, Major Schnaüfer arranged for his gunner, Wilhelm Gänsler, to move from East Germany, and he is still employed in the Schnaüfer family's wine business. Schnaüfer's was the only complete crew to be awarded Knight's Crosses in the entire Luftwaffe.

Their Me110 (No 720260) was evaluated by the RAF after the war, and was later included in a display of captured German aircraft in London's Hyde Park. It was eventually broken up, but one of its fins, showing Schnaüfer's tally of 121 victories, is displayed at the Imperial War Museum in London, whilst the other is in the Australian War Memorial Museum in Canberra.

Major Schnaüfer? After 121 victories from 164 night-fighter sorties, and emerging unscathed from the long conflict with Bomber Command, he was to meet his end in a car crash in France, in July 1950, victim of a French lorry with faulty brakes, surely one of the cruellest twists of fate.

He was a hero in anyone's language. But there is no accounting for fate.

E Erks

165 'Elevenses'. Queues were an everyday part of life even for service personnel in wartime Britain. No matter what you did or where you went on the station, it seemed you had to join the inevitable queue! You began the day by queuing at the wash-house, not quite awake, eyes distinctly red-rimmed, mouth and tongue feeling like leather; then you joined the none too enthusiastic throng at the cookhouse and wondered what gastronomic delights the cooks had in store. Mid-morning, while doing your DIs, you queued again when the 'Sally Ann' or YMCA tea van came to your dispersal, as illustrated here at Dunholme Lodge in April 1944. These No 44 (Rhodesia) Squadron lads wait patiently for a welcome 'cuppa' and a wad, seemingly not in talkative mood. Behind them, still with nose and engine covers on, stands BIII ND578 'KM:Y', then relatively new but destined to tot up 123 ops by VE-Day. She would pass to No 75 (New Zealand) Squadron at Spilsby before being declared surplus to requirements during the last days of October 1945. *E..E. Whitehouse*

165

The Toilers Far Below

Those who flew were not alone,
Behind them stood the friends unknown;
The fitters working day and night,
Their chief reward an A1 kite;
The riggers working hard to heal
The damage done by flying steel;
The armourers who handled tons
Of bombs, and laboured on the guns;
WAAFs who drove the transports round,
All the toilers on the ground;
Bowser drivers, cookhouse 'bods',
A thousand willing 'odds' and 'sods';
Supporting by their skill and care
Operations in the air.

Philip A. Nicholson

166, 167   Two of the Best. Early morning bustle at Faldingworth with engine fitters of the Polish-manned No 300 ('Masovian') Squadron performing their daily inspections. Normally operating in pairs, you engine mechs would each need around three hours to complete your allotted DIs — providing, of course, there were no major problems to overcome. Your programme of inspection, adjustment and rectification included such vital actions as checking of pipes and connections, oil filters, coolant, and exhaust stubs, and in normal weather conditions you would not mind working some fifteen feet high on open dispersals. Picture, however, the same exercise in the teeth of a cold blow sweeping in from the North Sea, or rain beating down like stair rods. Your face, barely visible beneath several layers of Balaclavas, would be screwed up in torment, numbed fingers on mittened hands grappling with ice-cold bolts and pipes and panels, curses largely muted and beyond the hearing of others more sensitive to disortions of the King's English! Ever adaptable, you were a colourful bunch, in the main men with a background of engineering in Civvy Street, men who loved your job despite the hardships, and who formed close ties with your aircrew during their tour, able and willing to tune their prized cars and provide illicit petrol. How, they ask, *did* you get rid of the pink dye? There was talk of ingenious stills on some squadrons but few aircrew asked too many questions! *Both Polish Sources*

168   Clipped-Wing Goose. This BII, 'EQ:U' (believed to be DS614) of No 408 ('Goose') Squadron RCAF in embarrassing attitude at Linton-on-Ouse calls to mind many adventures for those of you who did your stint on crash crew. How often your turn came round depended on your squadron, your CO, and it did not pay you to complain or you could find yourself on too many fire picket or funeral party duties! If your squadron had a busy night you would feel the effects of your labours for days. Before the introduction of air-filled bags you really had to slog, cutting and carving, winching and dragging out kites which bellied-in on the 'drome or ended up in fields and bogs nearby (those further afield you gladly left to the MU boys). Dunlop's flotation bags took much of the sweat and toil out of the job. You found that each bag, of seven cubic feet capacity, was capable of lifting a 12ton load and four could raise a Lancaster four feet in eight minutes, an unbelievable feat of engineering for those days. An apparent lack of activity suggested by our picture belies a certain amount of graft these and other erks will put in before the Lanc is returned to active squadron strength. Imagine a man in full flying gear: Mae West, parachute and harness, sometimes a thick fleece-lined leather suit, trying to make a rapid exit through the seemingly tiny escape hatch above the wings, more often than not in the dark, possibly under fire. In emergencies, such as the situation depicted here, however, it took mere seconds for several crew members to get out!
R. J. Fraser

168

169 King's Horses. Before you joined your squadron the chances are that you had never even seen a Merlin; or, at best, your knowledge of it was basic, mainly theoretical to say the least. At your trade-training school you had filled notebook after notebook with a thousand facts and figures relating to the theory of flight and hydraulics, propellers and other equally boring subjects by the score. Had you not spent hours drawing electrical and hydraulic circuits for the Merlin and Hercules — and for just about every engine in daily use with the RAF — until you knew them blindfold! When you did get your hands on a real engine it was usually a Kestrel, perhaps a Pegasus. Not that it mattered for you had yet to learn what engine would become the centre of your daily life. That you were posted to a Merlin-Lancaster unit was purely by chance, or luck, whatever the system or demand at the time decreed. You certainly did not regret it for no finer engine surely ever existed? Merlin — an inspiring name if ever there was one, whose very sound still grips you by the throat all these years later. Study anew this Packard-Merlin 224 (fitted to a No 431 ('Iroquois') Squadron RCAF Lanc X at Croft) with all cowlings removed to reveal the neat, compact, installation. You knew them as power eggs, weighing in at around one ton, attached to each nacelle bulkhead by just four bolts, and you could, working as a team of four, remove and fit a Merlin and prop in some four/six hours (depending on facilities — and co-operation from gremlins!). The picture shows the prop in fully-feathered position, ie, edge of blade into airstream to minimise drag in the event of an engine having to be shut down. *Public Archives of Canada*

170 Job for the Boys. Of all the day-to-day tasks you engine fitters performed on your squadron or con unit, perhaps the one you disliked most was priming the Ki-gas pumps situated inside each undercarriage well. Always the fear was with you that some clot in the cockpit would accidentally knock the undercart retraction lever; or that the undercart would collapse through structural failure. Even though accidents were few and far between, the fear never left you. As here, early morning action at 'sunny' Scampton, October/December 1942, starting up the starboard-inner of No 57 Squadron's 'DX:N' — you followed standard practice and worked as a team of three. While one of you manned the Ki-gas pumps, another sat in the cockpit to operate engine starting buttons and keep an eye open for mag drops and monitor temperature and pressure readings. Making up the trio, keeping watch to avoid fellow mortals walking into the lashing props was your corporal or any fitter handy. Whether clad in shoes, boots or, as is more likely, gum boots, you had no easy climb hauling yourself up greasy oleo legs and tyres. It could be a day of drizzle or of snow, your feet caked in mud or slippery with slush, and it did not help that each mainwheel tyre lacked any tread. The wet grass wouldn't make life any easier: not a hardstanding or 'pan' to be seen at this early stage of Lanc operations. *V. S. Moore*

171, 172 Graft and Gubbins. How soon you got through your DIs depended a great deal, of course, on how your aircrew had fared on ops the night before. You generally knew whether your kite had returned through spending the night as one of a duty crew, or by word of mouth filtering its way to your billet during the small hours. If actually out at the flights yourself you would have an uneasy time listening for your kite's call sign on the radio rigged up in your dispersal shack. It was a hollow feeling that she and her crew were overdue, their dispersal bay ominously empty while all around you came the noise of engines and human life as the squadron returned. You never quite got used to it, though, heaven knows, you experienced it again and again. You vowed never to get close to another crew, would keep your distance and counsel in future . . . yet, within a week or so you would warm to the replacement crew and were again on the path to heartache and sorrow. On mornings when you were aware your kite had returned you cycled down to the flights not knowing what to expect. Were she peppered with flak or bullet holes, whatever, your initial reaction was perhaps one of annoyance. You knew her every nut and bolt, every creak and groan, had nursed her as lovingly as you would were she your own . . . and you faced a long toil putting her

back to operational order. This feeling of annoyance quickly passed when you thought of the aircrew and their well-being.

Separated by 18 months and two counties are these typical morning-after-the-night-before studies. (171) Activity aplenty at Croft, winter 1944/5 as Iroquois erks prepare one of their charges. Remember those trolley accs, the drab-painted motor bikes and oxygen supply flat-top trucks . . . and all that mud! (172) Almost encircled by a confusion of teetering gantries at Binbrook stands BIII W5005 'AR:E²' of No 460 Squadron RAAF, already a veteran of 52 ops and destined to tot up 94 (and 606 flying hours) before Flt Sgt R. ('Hoppy') Hopman RAAF and his No 550 Squadron crew finished a trip to Kiel, 26-27 August 1944 by seeing rather too much of the Humber Estuary! *A. N. Mercer; E. D. Evans*

173, 174 Ins and Outs. (173) A section of Waddington definitely lacking in pastoral effect, with an armourer busily engaged in cleaning the .303in Brownings of No 467 Squadron RAAF BI PB754 'PO:U', using the standard pull-rods of the period and with an ample supply of 'four by twos' at his feet. This armourer has clearly barely begun his DIs for the mid-upper turret still has its cover tied in place, while only one pair of machine guns is installed and no doubt the other brace lie just out of view. As an air gunner you were not always obliged to clean your own guns. It depended on the individual, your squadron, your gunnery leader, your attitude to pride and personal satisfaction. During your tour you *were*, in conjunction with your fellow gunner, responsible for your kite's guns as survival could — and often did — hinge on their ability to operate freely and not jam or freeze up. As a crew you well knew your responsibilities — you were a team dependent on each other and, even if on your squadron it was the practice for amourers to clean your guns, you would generally assist — especially when it came to harmonising out on dispersal. You would on occasions serve in the armoury, helping hard-pressed armourers load the 14,000 rounds of .303s required by each Lancaster; or simply take your turn, on a rotation basis, stripping and assembling and generally familiarising yourself with the duties and problems of the armoury team. It all helped forge links. Before passing, it is interesting to record the fate of PB754 for the purists among you. She was wrecked at Bari, Italy, 17 August 1945 (then with No 35 Squadron), when Lancaster I ME834 of No 115 Squadron swung on take-off for the UK, on a return 'Dodge' trip, and ploughed into a row of parked aircraft. Also written off was another Lanc from 115: HK798. *D. Mason*

(174) Exemplifying the decidedly basic interior of a typical 'section' to be found on a wartime Lancaster station, we have three No 207 Squadron armourers intent on drawing such warmth as would be emitted by those diabolical stoves you all remember so well! Study the mud-spattered gum boots and you can gather what conditions were like out on the Bottesford flights during the winter of 1941/2. *G. Bentley*

174

*Late evening, a remote dispersal
On the airfield's edge;
Beyond the tarmac, unmown grass,
A distant line of trees, a hedge.*

*It could be just a picnic site,
A place to linger, sniff the summer air,
Admire the view; it could be,
But for that winged monster there.*

*Reminding us that we are off to war,
That soon we must be gone from here;
Must turn away from this green plot of peace,
To cross the fiery field of hate and fear.*

Philip A. Nicholson

175, 176   Gut Feeling. Less than one hour before take-off and with all external and internal checks done and everything in order, there is yet time for you to enjoy a smoke with your No 405 ('Vancouver') Squadron RCAF aircrew grouped beneath the towering bulk of 'LQ:V' at Gransden Lodge, probably 26 November 1943 before Berlin. Around you the dying embers of another day; scurrying clouds mask a pale sun soon to bid farewell, its tepid heat rapidly cooled by the chill of an oncoming late autumnal night. Your talk will cover a multitude of subjects — anything but the trip ahead — and never will the target be named. Despite a firm, unwavering bond between you fitters, riggers, armourers and your aircrew, you will not probe beyond the accepted bounds of security. You already have a rough idea from the petrol and bomb load . . . and to you all trips are the same for you will spend an anxious night awaiting return of *your* crew and *your* kite.

Take your place at Spilsby one crisp autumn day in 1943 and flood your mind with Merlin. Join the groundcrew who service 'F-Freddie' and listen as skipper Ken Letford exercises all four Merlins in unison. Maybe you never knew Spilsby or No 207 Squadron? Nor, too, does Lanc III ED586 'EM:F' mean anything to you . . . or that she finally went down on Stettin 5-6 January 1944 with Flt Lt G. H. Ebert and crew? But certain it is you remember the voice of Wynford Vaughan Thomas flying in her with Ken Letford and crew from Langar, recording his impressions four miles high over Berlin, 3-4 September 1943. That historic one-sided '78' was, you learn, cut in wax by a BBC sound engineer sat cramped in the rear fuselage of ED586 and is now a collectors' item. Whenever it is played on some radio request programme you stop whatever you are doing . . . and hear it through.
Public Archives of Canada; W. C. T. Bray

176

Elements

177

177 Another Day is Dying. That time of day — late afternoon or early evening — when the whole countryside is bathed in soft and filtered sunlight, the clouds as though painted on a huge backcloth of blue. There is an all-pervading hushed and brooding atmosphere with barely a whisper of wind and sound; perhaps the lone flapping of an engine cover on a nearby Lancaster or the steady monotonous note of a farm tractor in a distant field. Each Lancaster appears to 'dance' under the shimmering heat haze, wings and fuselage as well as cockpit and turret Perspex reflecting the rays of a summer sun, now dipping ever closer toward the horizon. They may have stood all day, you labouring groundcrews not always appreciating the intolerably hot interior, until you are through and soon the aircrew take over. As our picture was taken at Linton-on-Ouse some time in 1944, and features No 408 ('Goose') Squadron RCAF BIIs at rest, it could well be the end of an eventful day following a daylight venture. *R. J. Russell*

178 Mud-Lark. It is all too easy to think of airfields as open plains of lush, freshly mown grass on warm sunny days . . . of wide expanses of green flecked with daisies and buttercups, still and tranquil, seemingly empty of life save for the subdued humming of sleepy insects, the occasional cry of a bird. In reality they were more often than not a morass of grey unyielding mud, rather like a gigantic running sore, which seemed to cling to everything it touched and gave forth to some colourful expletives voiced by you groundcrews slipping and sliding ankle deep in the slime . . . thankful at least for your 'issue' gum boots. Indeed, many of you are reputed to have slept in your gum boots, so long were you forced to wear them during periods of inclement weather! Of you aircrew it can be said that many who completed your tour during the months of autumn and winter recall only endless days and nights of incessant rain and mist, fog and ice, wild and biting winds. Thus, our picture of No 106 Squadron's BI R5492 'ZN:S' surrounded by mud at Syerston, 28 November 1942, may bring back rather unpleasant memories. The snap was taken by air gunner Sgt Vic Della Porta prior to his first op' — Turin 28-29 November 1942 — with Sgt Vic Hayward as skipper. Witness the firing butts visible beyond the Lanc's nose; also the hangar — both still there at defunct Syerston today. Like so many crews of the period the Hayward seven paid the ultimate price, not returning from Wilhelmshaven 11-12 February 1943, while R5492's demise is shrouded in mystery: when serving with No 1661 HCU she crashed near Exeter on the night of 3-4 September 1943, engaged on local defence exercises. She was one of the earliest production Lancs, delivered in February 1942 after starting life on the AVRO assembly line as a Manchester. Her crudely-painted codes do not hide the evidence of earlier service with No 44 (Rhodesia) Squadron as 'KM:M', her shabby, workworn appearance matching the surroundings.
V. E. Della Porta

Men For All Seasons

Fickle as a young girl's heart,
Weather played a vital part.
Forecast winds could change and veer,
A navigator's constant fear.
In spite of every new device
All crews feared the demon ice.
Downstairs, if shrouding fog came down
"Ops are cancelled, off to town!"
Remember, too, those luckless types,
The ground crews who, despite their gripes,
Worked through winters foul and grim
To keep their precious Lancs in trim.
But there were times of awed surprise
As towering cloudscapes filled the skies;
And sunsets when the climbing kite
Glowed crimson in the fading light.

Philip A. Nicholson

179, 180   Chilled and Stilled. Picturesque maybe, worthy of selection as suitable Christmas cards were they not taken in wartime. Chilling scenes like these at Skellingthorpe (179) and Waddington (180) you would not always appreciate. You knew only too well that it meant clearing runways, hard-standings and the like at a time when you could be better employed exercising your right arm, or, worse still, when you should be enjoying some well-earned beauty sleep. Whilst on rare occasions would an overnight mantle of snow hold up your station's flying programme for more than a few hours, there *were* exceptions and many of you will recall the severe winter of 1943/4 in particular, which virtually paralysed the whole of 'bomber country' from the uplands and dales of Durham and Yorkshire to the fens and plains of Cambridge and Hunts for several weeks. While you aircrew would

welcome the break from operations you would none-the-less be required to take your turn with broom and shovel and join in the exhausting graft. At least these enforced stand-downs had the attraction of 'hitting' the local hosteleries in the evenings — providing the beer did not run out! Our Skellingthorpe picture features a No 50 Squadron Lanc during the bitter winter of 1943/4, with hydraulic jack propping up her starboard wing while awaiting fitment of a new undercart. In our second view No 467 Squadron RAAF Lancs, drawn up line abreast at Waddington during the same winter, have little to fear from intruders with Allied and Axis air operations brought to a standstill. 'PO:L' is BI DV277, which would be scrapped at No 46 MU Lossiemouth, November 1946.
A. L. Bartlett; J. A. Colpus

181 Winter Fare. Croft on one of those days when the whole of England is clamped by weather so bad that even the birds are grounded. The countryside takes on a drab coat of grey beneath a canopy of low clag, ever changing its form, clinging and unfriendly. It is a day when you sit in the flight office huddled by the stove, hands cupped around mugs of hot sticky tea, maybe discussing what you are all going to do once this bind of a war is over and behind you; or, for those who cannot see that far ahead (or even want to), outlining plans for the next 'bash' at Betty's Bar in York, or the Imperial or Freemason's Arms in Darlington (unless it is girls you are after then you will head for the Fleece!). Despite all this there is as yet no stand-down, for the Allied Armies are pushing the Axis farther towards the Fatherland and the weather may yet lift and result in another urgent call for assistance from the heavies. Thus, work must continue out on the flights. There is a multitude of everyday tasks to be done so no rest for duty riggers and fitters effecting repairs to bomb doors, control surfaces and generally patching up results of flak or fighter damage received the day or night before. Once through, and all kites ground run they, too, can repair to their shacks, there to loosen up stiffened limbs while enjoying a brew-up. Some idea of conditions on such a day can be gauged from our picture of Croft under the grip of winter early in 1945, a wilderness of icy pools and ruts so treacherous underfoot. Foreground is a No 434 ('Bluenose') Squadron RCAF kite being ground run. *M. Bachinski*

Extinction

182 The Sun Sets Everyday for Someone. You had barely known death before you donned RAF blue. The nearest you had been to death was attending the funeral of an aged aunt òr some other member of your family or friend or neighbour. Such deaths as you had known were due to age or illness, were somehow acceptable and had an air of respectability about them. A few of you had, it is true, seen another kind of death — those due to coal mine disasters for instance — but for most of you there was a rude awakening ahead. You quickly touched death during your early months of learning. As you progressed through pilot training, navigation school, wherever, there was the inevitable toll of crashes through bad weather or inexperience, even worn-out aircraft; it had a sobering effect. The hard realities of war usually greeted you as you settled in to your squadron Nissen hut. If the MPs were not clearing out the gear of a missing crew as you moved in — you had been allotted *their* beds! — you soon knew of the distasteful duty performed by the Committee of Adjustment (usually including the Padre and Adjutant). Within days of your ensconcement you would awaken one morning to find empty beds opposite you; or, on your return from leave you could find yourself the sole occupant of your hut. For many of your number it would be *your* bed among those empty the following day!

This funeral procession took place at Faldingworth and relates to a Polish crew who died when their No 300 ('Masovian') Squadron Lancaster crashed on return from an operation. There would be an interring of a very different nature for those who did not return — if indeed their bodies were ever recovered. *D. Gowin*

182

123

183 A Life to Remember. Long after you have forgotten the meaning of AMOs, DROs, and an endless array of forms and orders which seemd to rule your every day of service life, you remember Tee Emm. Officially the Royal Air Force's Training Memorandum, Tee Emm you found to be the one readable effort among the wads of bumph churned out with unlimited regularity and which you had to absorb. Through its telling essays you were continually reminded of your responsibilities, your need for constant awareness, attention to detail. Too easily could *you* be the subject of This Month's Prunery — The Most Highly Derogatory Order of the Irremovable Finger! . . . and other articles featuring Bill Hooper's Pilot Officer Prune. The graveyards were full of men who paid the price for being careless, over-confident, unfit to fly due to head colds . . . all putting their crew's lives in jeopardy. Here is a mock grave at Binbrook with its own message for the unwary. It purports to represent the body of a bomb aimer who died following failure to do a visual check on his bomb load and the headstone's verse carries a prophetic message. A hand-held mop partly hides the heading 'Lest You Forget' and an unknown poet has added these lines:

Here lies a bomb aimer who failed to select
And omitted to do his visual check
On landing his bombs blew him nearer to God
And the scraped up remains lie under this sod!

You wonder if it still stands at Binbrook today? *L. E. Aitken*

184

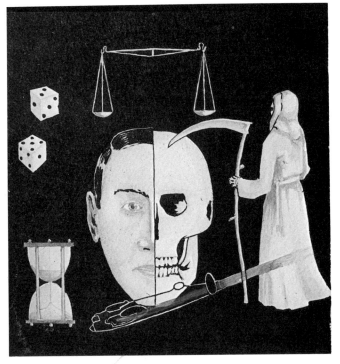

184, 185   The Fickle Hand of Fate. 'The chop' . . . 'Going for a Burton' . . . colourful phrases denoting the loss of a crew or an individual on operations and but two examples of a unique language coined during the war and having its own particular place in history. The men of Bomber Command — boys who became men in a few brutal nights — had to stare death in the face — even laugh at the prospect . . . at least outwardly. Each man had to believe it could not happen to him. Was *your* crew not careful and diligent, yet never over confident . . . and your skipper the best there was? Moreover, you believed in your task, were patriotic to a man (were there *really* some who revelled in it all?) . . . and, living for the day, your mantle of youth precluded thoughts of what tomorrow held.

(184) How an artist (from either No 61 or 617 Squadron) saw the fortunes of war relative to Lancaster aircrew. A pair of dice, scales, and an egg timer, all graphically illustrate the luck element, tipping of the scales against survival, sands of time running out . . . and there, awaiting your call, the Reaper. *J. E. R. Williams*

(185) Some squadrons even had their own exclusive 'club' for those who beat the chop. This is the front face of a membership card issued to No 207 Squadron (Spilsby) air gunners who survived the traumatic experience of being shot down, clearly recognised by the unit's CO. *R. T. Emeny*

185

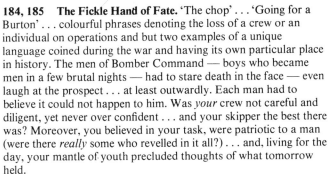

PATRON
W/C H.R.BLACK, A.F.C.
PRESIDENT
F/L J.WARDLE, D.F.M.

MEMBERSHIP CARD

186, 187 Heartache Beyond the Dawn. Telling pictures of typical No 5 Group Lancaster crashes, which, at times, seemed to litter the county of Lincolnshire. As the number of squadrons and conversion units increased, so, inevitably, did the prangs. Apart from the usual problems associated with converting from Wellingtons and Whitleys (the two types forming the backbone of the OTUs), the threat of total extinction or maiming for life awaited you on operations and routine training. Often tired to the point of exhaustion, and shot-up like collanders, you faced a multitude of hidden dangers. Mother Nature, too, in her many moods —

treacherous fog and ice, blinding snow and driving rain — pushed you to the limit. How 'basic' it all seems four decades later.

(186) A Lanc burnt out in a field adjoining Waddington some time in 1942 and revealing little for the subsequent Court of Inquiry. Note the anti-invasion posts. The second view (187) is dated 10 December 1943 and could be the result of an overshoot and ensuing ground loop, judging from position of tail section relative to main fuselage. More here for the investigators.
Both E. T. McCabe

126

188

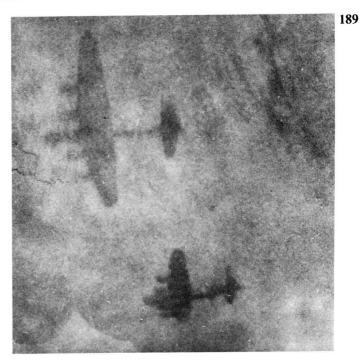

188-190   You Needed Luck. To see a Lancaster — indeed any bomber — blow up, be it laden with bombs or not, was an unforgettable experience. Hardened though you became in the course of a tour, you would still mentally and physically flinch on seeing seven of your number blown to oblivion. Up to a thousand pairs of eyes could watch the spectacle of flowering flame and black smoke — more often than not in total silence — until strict discipline demanded you avert your gaze and keep to the stark realities of the task ahead. Even so you fleetingly wondered whether you knew them, had drunk with them, had shared the same liberty bus. Seven youngsters just like your own crew, each with as much right as yourselves to see this war out, and make a life for themselves in the future. Seven highly trained aircrew, the cream of many a nation's youth, wiped out at a stroke; men who happened to be in the wrong place at the wrong time. It seemed so unfair, yet it could so easily be *your* crew, and you came to acknowledge the fact that your chances of survival shortened as your tour progressed, despite your experience. As young as you were you did not have to be a professor of maths to understand that ultimately the odds on not coming back were about even; that one in two of you had to die — how did not matter, the end was the same — and you hoped this uncertainty did not show in a lessening of confidence and trust in each other. Above all you had to consider it a job and live for the day. Tomorrow was another world. Tomorrow that missing crew's names would be erased from the blackboard, rarely to be mentioned again, their place quickly filled with replacements from the training pool.

This remarkable set of pictures records the demise of two Iroquois crews. (188 and 189) Looking through the cockpit canopy of a No 431 ('Iroquois') Squadron RCAF BX, a cloud of acrid smoke and debris is all that remains of a 30ton Lancaster: the Iroquois' CO, Wg Cdr R. F. Davenport RCAF and his all-Canadian crew, flying BX KB853 'SE:A' obliterated in an instant over Essen, 11 March 1945. *Both G. E. Kercher*

(190) From the astrodome of a No 434 ('Bluenose') Squadron RCAF BI (skipper: Flt Lt Warrie Rothenbush RCAF) Canadian wireless op Flg Off Neil Taschuk captures for evermore the last moments of BX KB808 'SE:Y' over Hildesheim, 22 March 1945. This time eight men died — made even more tragic as Flt Lt J. P. Duggan RCAF and crew (six Canucks and one British) were on their last trip of the tour. (The unlucky eighth man being a 'second dickey' pilot.) *N. G. Taschuk*

191-199 Agony for All. Does it anger you, fill you with shame each year as Remembrance Day approaches, you see any number of erstwhile volunteers rattling their collection boxes, shouldering their trays of poppies, ignored by too many shoppers? How many of you find it deplorable that Air Force Associations and Legions should be forced to rely on charity in order to provide comfort for debilitated veterans, dependents of those killed, educate their children? No-one will ever convince you successive governments have done enough for widows — indeed, next of kin generally. In Britain, if nowhere else, their plight was certainly highlighted by revelations made a year after the recent Falklands war. As much as you approved the announcement of generous gratuities and pensions resulting from that conflict (remuneration, of course, depended on a man's rank, his potential!), did you not consider it unjust that those whose actions were fought before 1972 should be excluded? Do you wonder how the widow of your tousle-haired gunner has fared? And the kin of others like him . . . lads who died violently and who too frequently have no known graves. Are you haunted still by the memory of visiting their families, feeling an imposter, distinctly uncomfortable . . . sensing their undoubted unspoken resentment? Why had *you* survived? Why was it not *their* boy sitting there facing them? Not that you regret making that visit. Had not all seven of you pledged yourselves to such an undertaking, whoever returned from POW camp . . . wherever, whenever? Not *your* crew? Then maybe you considered it necessary to bequeath personal belongings to each other in the event of your demise? It was not uncommon for you to make a pact with another crew on your station.

97 (Straits Settlements) Squadron
Royal Air Force,
Bourn, Cambridge.
31st March, 1944.

Dear Mr. Hyde,

It is with the deepest regret that I must confirm that your son, Flight Lieutenant L.V. Hyde, failed to return from night operations on the 30/31st March 1944, and I wish to express the sympathy of the whole Squadron with you in your anxiety.

Flight Lieutenant Hyde took part in a raid on Nuremburg as Pilot and Captain of the aircraft, no news having since been received. We can but hope that the aircraft was forced to land and that the crew are safe, even as prisoners of war.

Since your son joined the Squadron at the beginning of October last year, he has completed twenty-two successful sorties over enemy territory. He was a very experienced pilot and captain of one of our most reliable crews. They were therefore undertaking a leading role in the bombing offensive against the enemy. We miss him and his fellows and their loss is a sad blow to the Squadron.

It is desired to explain that the request in the telegram notifying you of the casualty to your son was included with the object of avoiding his chance of escape being prejudiced by undue publicity in case he was still at large. This is not to say that any information about him is available, but is a precaution adopted in the case of all personnel reported missing.

His kit and personal effects are being carefully checked and will be sent to the R.A.F. Central Depository, from whom you will hear in due course.

If any news is received I will communicate with you immediately, and in the meantime I join with you in hoping we shall soon hear that your son and his crew are safe.

Yours sincerely,

Wing Commander, Commanding,
No.97 (Straits Settlements)
Squadron, R.A.F. Bourn.
(E. J. Carter)

Mr. W. H. Hyde,
10, Queen's Avenue,
Shirley,
BIRMINGH M.

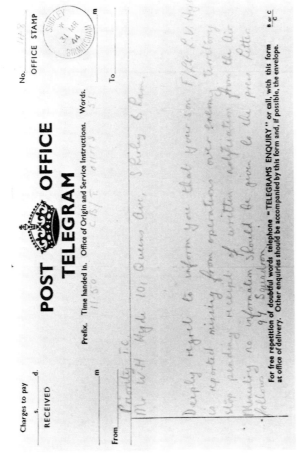

POST OFFICE TELEGRAM

At Spilsby for instance Flg Off Ren Watters of No 207 Squadron drew up a will (191) on officers' mess notepaper leaving his effects to close friend and fellow Kiwi skipper Flg Off Steve Roberton. Happily both survived to return home to New Zealand and are still firm friends today. For too many men there was no such happy ending. Too many widows, brothers, children are left with little more than fading medal ribbons . . . a handful of yellowing snapshots . . . log books whose entries end abruptly. And terse telegrams and stereotyped letters, as despatched by the thousand to too many homes. And here's a thought: how do you imagine each CO or flight commander, adjutant or padre felt, churning out those communiques with sickening regularity? *Someone* had to do it.

Will: D. R. Watters; Depository Letter: T. B. Waite;
All Other Letters: H. J. Hyde

195

Tel. No.
GERRARD 9234. Ext. ....

Correspondence on the subject of
this letter should be addressed to
THE UNDER-SECRETARY
OF STATE,
AIR MINISTRY (P.4(Cas.)).
and should quote the reference
P.415416/1/P.4.B.6.

Your Ref. ....

AIR MINISTRY,
73-77, OXFORD STREET,
LONDON. W.I.

August 1944

Sir,

I am directed to inform you, with deep regret,
that all efforts to trace your son, Acting Flight Lieutenant
L. V. Hyde, have proved unavailing.

In view of the absence of news for so long a
period, it is felt that you should be informed of this
Department's grave anxiety for his safety, but action to
presume that he has lost his life will not be taken until
evidence of his death is received, or until such time
has elapsed that it is considered there can be no longer
any likelihood of his survival.

Such action will then be for official purposes
only and will not be taken until this Department has
communicated with you further.

I am to assure you that all possible enquiries
are continuing.

I am, Sir,
Your obedient Servant,

for Director of Personal Services

W. H. Hyde Esq.,
10 Queens Avenue,
Shirley,
Birmingham.

194

Telephone Nos:-
COLNBROOK 231-232-233.

In reply please quote
reference:-
CD/

CENTRAL DEPOSITORY,
ROYAL AIR FORCE,
COLNBROOK,
SLOUGH, Bucks.

4. May

1163402 Lt. Waite, E.N.L.

Dear Sir,

The personal effects of your son, as listed on the
attached inventory have now reached this office from the Unit and will
be held in safe custody pending the receipt of further evidence which
will enable a conclusive classification of the casualty to be made.

In the case of casualties reported as "missing" unless
definite evidence comes to light in the meantime, authority to release
the effects is not normally received from the Air Ministry until at
least six months from the date of the casualty, since official action
to presume death is rarely taken before the expiration of this period.

In the case of casualties ultimately reported "Prisoner of
War" the Air Ministry will as a general rule, only authorise the release
of effects on the written request of the officer or airman concerned.
In these circumstances, in order to expedite release, any original letter
received from a Prisoner of War in this connection should be forwarded
to this office for perusal and early return.

In the meantime, may I be permitted to express my sympathy
with you in this period of anxiety.

Yours faithfully,

Squadron Leader, Commanding,
R.A.F. Central Depository.

J. Waite, Esq.,
2. Poplar Cottage,
Hereford Road,
Meole Brace,
SHREWSBURY.

TELEPHONE : GERRARD 9234
Extn.

Any communications on the subject of this letter should be addressed to :—
THE
UNDER SECRETARY
OF STATE,

and the following number quoted :— P.415416/1/P.4.Cas. B.4.

Your Ref. ....

AIR MINISTRY

(Casualty Branch),

73-77, OXFORD STREET,
W.1.

28th November 1944.

W.H. Hyde, Esq.,
10, Queens Avenue,
Shirley,
Birmingham.

Sir,

I am directed to refer to the letter dated 4th April, 1944, from the Department notifying you that your son, Acting Flight Lieutenant Leonard Victor Hyde, Royal Air Force, was reported missing as the result of air operations on the night of 30th/31st March, 1944, and to inform you, with regret, that although no definite news of your son has come to hand, a report regarding certain of the occupants of the aircraft has been received from the International Red Cross Committee.

This report, quoting German information, states that Flying Officer R.J. Weller, D.F.M., and three members, whose identity the German Authorities are unable to establish at present, all belonging to the crew of this Lancaster aircraft, lost their lives on 31st March, 1944.

As there were seven members in the crew, it will be appreciated that it is not possible to state precisely who are the three unidentified members but it is considered that you would wish to be notified of this report.

I am to add an expression of the Department's sympathy with you in your anxiety, and to assure you that you will be informed of any further news received.

I am, Sir,
Your obedient Servant,

for Director of Personal Services.

Tel. No.—Horoxxxx14, Sloane 3467
Ext. ....

Correspondence on the subject of this letter should be addressed to
THE UNDER-SECRETARY
OF STATE,
AIR MINISTRY,.............
and should quote the reference
P.415416/44/S.7.Cas.(b).2.

Your Ref. ....

AIR MINISTRY,

LONDONxxW6xx
(Casualty Branch),
2, Seville Street,
Knightsbridge,
S.W.1.

22 March, 1947.

Sir,

I am directed to refer to the loss of your son, Flight Lieutenant L.V. Hyde, D.F.C., and to say that while the Department is reluctant to re-open this painful subject it is felt that you would wish to know that information obtained from captured German documents has enabled the Missing Research and Enquiry Service of the Royal Air Force to institute a special investigation to establish the fate of your son and his crew.

These documents state that the aircraft in which they were flying was shot down at 12.30 a.m. on the 31st March, 1944, one kilometre west of Nunchholzhausen, near Wetzlar and that four members of the crew, Flying Officer Weller and three whose identity could not be established, were found dead. Of these four, two were buried at Lutzellinden and two at Nunchholzhausen.

The Research Service are accordingly endeavouring to ascertain the fate of the three members of the crew who so far remain untraced and to establish the identity of the three buried as "unknown".

Although it may be some while before the investigations are completed I am to assure you that you will be notified as soon as the result becomes available.

I am, Sir,
Your obedient Servant,

W.H. Hyde, Esq.,
10, Queens Avenue,
Shirley,
Birmingham.

198

P41C416/314 Cas/C?

AIR MINISTRY,
2, SEVILLE STREET,
LONDON, S.W.1.
4 December, 1947.

Dear Mr. Hyde,

I am very sorry to renew your grief in the sad loss of your son Flight Lieutenant L.V. Hyde, but I am sure you will wish to know of a report which has now been received from the Royal Air Force Missing Research and Enquiry Service in Germany concerning the fate of his aircraft and crew.

The Search Officers' investigations have confirmed that the aircraft crashed at Muncholzhausen near Wetzlar, and that all members of the crew, who must have been killed instantly, were buried by the Germans in the cemeteries at Muncholzhausen and Lutzellinden. Individual identification has been possible in the case of two occupants of the graves, of which your son is, unfortunately, not one, and their remains have been reverently reinterred in the British Military Cemetery at Hannover (Limmer), where he now rests in a comrades' group of graves numbered 1 to 5 in Row E Plot 8, with the four other members of his crew who also could not be individually identified.

I must explain that this policy of reburial has been agreed upon by His Majesty's and the Commonwealth Governments because it is felt that our fallen should not be left in isolated cemeteries throughout Germany, but should rest together in special military cemeteries, the soil of which will always be British. These cemeteries, which have been selected for the natural beauty and peace of their surroundings, will be tended

/in

W.H. Hyde, Esq.,
10, Queens Avenue,
Shirley,
Birmingham.

199

in perpetuity by the Imperial War Graves Commission.

The Commission will consult you later on regarding the inscription upon the headstone they will erect to his memory, and a photograph of the graves will also be sent to you, although I am afraid this will not be for some considerable time.

I do sincerely hope the knowledge that your son's last resting place with those of his comrades surrounding it, will always be reverently tended, may be of some slight comfort to you.

Yours sincerely,

[signature]

200-201 A Sidelong Look. When, on Remembrance Day each year you pay your respects to those who gave their all, be it on parade or in the privacy of your home, you naturally give special thought to crews you knew and who didn't make it. It is the one time in the year when maybe you pull out the old log book and album . . . and remember. So many faces . . . so many names . . . men, just like you, full of hopes and ideals; men who died never to feel a furrowed brow, a thinning head of hair, never to know the joy of their children's laughter; men, once a fine balance of sinew and bone and muscle and blood; men who talked and laughed and thought and wondered and were afraid. All the memorials in the world cannot recapture their spirit, their gaiety, their courage, their unselfishness. So, too, do a range of index cards recording Lancaster production in a Ministry filing system on their own mean nothing. Only when linked with the mortals who manned them, so often died in them, are they meaningful. Take R5741 and ED700, just two of 3,349 Lancs which ended their brief span of life as funeral pyres. Neither R5741 nor ED700 survived and are little more than typed entries in weighty tomes at the Public Records Office, Kew, taking their place alongside the deeds of Drake and Nelson, for aeons to come.

(200) BI R5741 'OF:K' of No 97 (Straits Settlements) Squadron, Woodhall Spa and flown by WO Maurice Cullinane RCAF and crew for 10 ops but which failed to make it back from Saarbrucken, 1-2 September 1942 (with fellow Canadian Flt Sgt R. H. Morgan

and crew) while they were on leave. 'Cully' Cullinane and several of his crew went on to complete two tours and become members of an exclusive club. *S. W. Archer*

(201) No 9 Squadron's BIII ED700 'WS:O' kept going for almost eight months before she sank to the bottom of the North Sea on return from Frankfurt, 20-21 December 1943. Aboard that night was as fated a crew as you could meet: Plt Off E. J. Argent and his boys were forever in trouble and finally went down on Brunswick, 14-15 January 1944. Bardney was still unfinished when Sqn Ldr Dickie Bunker taxied her out for one of the four attacks on Hamburg known to history as Operation 'Gomorrah'. Long after ED700 and Dickie Bunker have left us, Bardney is still recognisable as an airfield. Ignore the skeletal remains of a postwar missile site at the intersection of two runways and work your way round the peritrack until you locate this spot. . . . *J. Batchelor Collection*

200

201

202-203 They, Too, Needed Luck. You saw enough during your first five ops — your so-called apprenticeship term — to realise you were going to need luck — lots of it — if you were to survive your tour. Already, during that first fortnight, month — the span depended on the period you were operating — yours might be the lone survivor of two, even three crews who joined the squadron the very same day. Crews no less qualified, no less proficient than your own, gone, barely remembered. So might you all survive to be tour expired within a few days of one another. There was no pattern. Death — total oblivion — you soon learned, was totally indiscriminate. So it was with the aircraft you flew and maintained. Where one Lanc would disappear within days — sometimes hours of arriving on squadron, another would survive for a whole year, be she patched, re-engined, have new wings, tail, whatever it took to keep her flying. Two such veterans were BIII ED593 and BI LL806, each of which saw the war out, albeit ED593 by then grounded as instructional airframe 4944M at Lindholme, and LL806 demoted to squadron hack. ED593 'ZN:Y', named *Admiral Prune II* totted up at least 72 ops with No 106 Squadron before being pensioned off, while ED592 and ED594, built on the same AVRO Chadderton production line, managed but 115 hours between them. (ED592 joined No 50 Squadron 7 February 1943 and met her end on Berlin, 1-2 March; ED594 of No 57 Squadron blew up at Scampton 15 March 1943.)

No 15 Squadron's LL806, 'LS:J', amassed 134 ops, plus three 'Manna' and three 'Exodus' sorties, yet the combined total hours of LL805 and LL807, produced by Armstrong Whitworth the same day, was no more than 60. (LL805, with No 15 Squadron from 21 April 1944, failed to return from Friedrichshaven, 27-28 April of the same month; LL807 went down on Gelsenkirchen, 12-13 June 1944 when with No 300 ('Masovian') Squadron). Nose close-up is of LL806 at home base Mildenhall mid-1945. Three-quarter front shot is of ED593 at Syerston late summer 1943. To think that one day those gracious elms would themselves be threatened!
D. A. Russell; V. G. Adams

Faces Glimpsed and Never Seen Again

Boys in the company of boys,
They died before they had lived;
Shot, blown apart, consumed in fire,
Broken in shattered wreckage;
Despatched with indignity
And without preparation.
I mourned them then,
But now, surviving in a world
Indifferent to their hopes and dreams,
I grieve more for the living.

Philip A. Nicholson

204   Seven for a Secret. Always you faced death at the hands of a resourceful, tenacious enemy. You accepted, too, that at any time you could perish due to inclement weather . . . your own inexperience . . . your lack of vigilance . . . running out of luck. But did it ever occur to you that you might die due to faulty workmanship, incompetence, even sabotage? Of course not! But happen it did now and then. And when it did you found it obscene, totally unacceptable. Take what happened to Flt Sgt Sid Chapman RAAF and crew. Does this snap, of them posing with their beloved *Liz'beth* (BIII LM311 'PO:L') help those of you with No 467 Squadron RAAF at Bottesford, summer 1943, to remember them? It does for Cliff Allen, engine fitter, and his words tell you far more than any official report ever can:

'I will always remember that morning, 13 July 1943. The first Lanc back from Turin landed about 08.30am. Maxie and I had gone to breakfast. "L-Love" was very late. (I didn't work on "PO:L" myself but my friend Maxie Byrne was rigger on her.) We had started to eat when "Tubby" Murray (Aussie) came rushing in (Maxie's Sergeant). "L-Love" had crashed and he wanted help in lifting wreckage off the body of the pilot, Flt Sgt Chapman. We didn't hesitate and were joined by Stan Locking, a mech off "B-Beer". A truck took us to a field near the scene of the crash about a mile from the 'drome.

' "L-Love" had crashed in a cornfield almost ready for cutting. We could see a pall of black smoke and as we made toward the wreck through a swathe in the corn there was a sudden downpour. It came down in torrents. What we saw wasn't a pleasant sight I might add, and one of the boys was sick.

'When we arrived at the scene of the wreckage the only recognisable part of the Lanc was a section of the fuselage aft of the wireless op's cabin. This had been split wide open and we could see the rest bed, which was still intact. Sitting on this in an upright position was the body of the flight engineer who was badly charred. Tubby Murray called us over to a section of mainplane which he wanted lifting. A mobile crane was standing by and when our efforts brought no result this was hooked on to the jagged metal and it lifted the mainplane to one side.

'It was still raining heavily and craters caused through the debris were soon deep puddles filled with oily water, pieces of metal and wire. Here and there remains of maps, the odd coin and minced-up flesh. Personnel from the sick-bay were trying to identify remains and label them. I went round what I thought was the front of the aircraft and then I saw the yellow tips of the airscrew blades just visible out of the ground. I remember remarking to Maxie that the engines must be 10ft in the ground. Tubby had found the armour-plating shield which was fixed behind the pilot's seat. This was compressed level to the ground and we all recognised it by the yellow gas-warning disc painted on it. The crane-hook was attached and after much tearing of metal it began to lift, bringing with it the pilot's seat. The torso of skipper Chapman was the only remains left. Now all the crew had been accounted for and after making the area safe to move about in we left.

'When I think back I often wonder if the engines were ever lifted out of the ground. One day I'll go back and see if I can find the location of this crash. I still think of that crew, how near they were to safety and how they all must have been up front in the aircraft because of the dangerous state of the tail-section.

'We completed our task and the tragic end of LM311 has always remained in my memory more than any other war-time experience. I remember this series of Lancs being grounded for investigation. "L-Love" hadn't been damaged by enemy action and we were told later it was due to inferior riveting in the tail section. This section dropped off immediately the undercarriage was lowered. The pilot had called for an emergency landing but had to do another circuit owing to another Lanc being given an emergency landing.

'The name *Liz'beth* on the nose of LM311 "PO:L" was, incidentally, the name of Flt Sgt Chapman's girl friend, a WAAF transport driver. Unfortunately she happened to be on duty that morning and would have been collecting the crew of "L-Love". We all felt for her after the crash as they had planned to marry in the near future'.

What happened to the Chapman crew sent ripples of anger and disbelief throughout the Command. By immediately grounding all Lancasters in the same A. V. Roe Yeadon production batch, there was, too, the need to suppress ugly rumours spreading — and fast. Fortunately this was achieved and the faults at the factory were quickly overcome. Like all aircraft produced under wartime conditions, the Lancaster was not without its share of problems in the shape of sabotage, incompetence, and poor workmanship. Thankfully, instances were very few . . . but the loss of LM311 was not, unhappily, to be the last. *C. Allen*

Corkscrew Starboard — Go!

Ray Harris

Fear was ever-present during operations. Don't believe anyone who says he was not afraid. Sure, there were varying degrees of fear, but it was there. Flying itself added its own dimension to the stress of operational life, whilst the constant probability of being shot-at considerably heightened the degree of apprehension with which men just had to live. Actually being fired-at turned controlled or suppressed fear into instant stark terror, which set even the supposedly bravest of men white and shaking. It is said a man does not know himself until he has been shot-at.

Being fired on is a horrific experience, as any serviceman will confirm. However much you trained for the event, or however tough you thought you were, nothing could diminish the fear of being hit, wounded — perhaps maimed for life. For aircrew there was the additional fear of plunging to earth from miles high. That was the third dimension — probably the worst.

On night ops, it tended to be an instant thing — a sudden hit, or near-miss from flak; or an equally sudden burst of cannon fire from an unseen fighter, below or behind. In daylight it was different, as the American B-17 and B-24 boys had found. You could see the fighters coming, and from the flak pattern, knew when it was your turn. It was, in one word: terrifying; yet there was little you could do but grit your teeth and force yourself to aim, and fire back, gaining some comfort from the sheer numbers of guns flying along with you.

Imagine being caught on your own — a singleton in flying parlance — on a clear day; a sitting duck. The terror is unimaginable to those who have never experienced drama in the air. Even with the heaviest of armament, or most skilled of gunners, a lone bomber is virtually defenceless against fighters. Yet miraculously, some survived just such an ordeal, and lived to tell the tale.

The story which follows concerns a highly experienced crew, already with 32 operations to its credit, in a tour which had begun $7\frac{1}{2}$ months previously, a week before D-Day, 1944:

'Four Mustangs approaching on the starboard bow, Skipper.' The routine voice of Bill Gabriel, the rear gunner, broke intercom silence as the Lancaster, mission accomplished and much lighter now, headed out across the Norwegian coastline for the long journey home. The pilot held a steady course, and brooded. Why were they so late? The missing fighter escort of Polish Mustangs should have been waiting above the target area to protect his aircraft should enemy fighters appear. None had, though the U-boat pens had been well armed with anti-aircraft guns. The navigator handed him his traditional Woodbine. It was a post-objective ritual he usually relaxed to enjoy. He inhaled deeply, nervously, worried. 'If they were going to be so late,' he asked himself, 'then why the hell bother to turn up at all?'

In the rear gun turret, Flt Lt Bill Gabriel was asking himself the same question. He had been on many similar sorties, against strongly defended targets, but the escorts were usually waiting, keen and punctual. It was odd for them to arrive so late — especially the Poles. Thoughtfully he watched the approaching fighters. The Mustangs were much closer now, squat, purposeful and efficient, heading straight towards them, almost within fighting range, almost like . . . suddenly he stared more closely, gasped, and then at last he understood.

'Christ!' shouted the mid-upper — he had seen it too — 'they're bloody '190s!'

Their warning came over the intercom in sudden urgent unison: 'Corkscrew starboard — go!' Two seconds later the first shattering salvo of Luftwaffe cannon shells slammed into the side of the Lancaster, and their world seemed to explode from within.

It was at breakfast time on 12 January 1945, at No 9 Squadron, Bardney, near Lincoln, that Flt Lt Ray Harris had learned from the Battle Order posted in the mess that he and his crew had been chosen as wind-finders for the day's operation. He strolled over with the other pilots to the briefing room. He was small, fair-haired, and little more than 20. It was to be his 33rd mission, and the crew list was: Pilot, Flt Lt R. J. (Ray) Harris RAFVR; Nav, Flt Sgt F. W. ('Doc') Young RAFVR; F/E, Sgt M. (Maurice) Mellors RAFVR; W/OP, Flg Off W. R. (Bill) Brownlie RAFVR; P/O, Flt Off H. F. C. (Jimmy) Parsons RAFVR; M/U, Plt Off A. J. ('Mac') MacWilliams RAFVR; R/G, Flt Lt W. T. G. (Bill) Gabriel RAFVR.

The target was the U-boat pens at Bergen, in enemy-occupied Norway, and the plan was simple. They would take-off at 08.46, a few minutes before the rest of the squadron, bomb the submarine pens at 13.00hrs, and be home in time for tea. An escort of Mustang fighters from a nearby Polish squadron would be over the target to protect them.

The crew would be taking 'their own' Lanc, BI PD198, 'WS-W', christened *Willing Winnie*, which they had taken over from new for their 11th op in mid-July 1944. She had already served them well, this to be their 18th trip with her.

The three-hour flight was uneventful, and they were looking down at the concrete pens a good five minutes before the main force arrived. Anti-aircraft guns opened up to welcome them, but the sky was clear. There was no sign of the promised escort.

The pilot flew over the target in a wide triangle, while the navigator calculated wind speed and direction and transmitted the information back to the main force for the

205-206 **Winnie's Boys.** The King's Commission, pilot's wings and a DFC: Ray Harris — a veteran at 21. Ray's Lanc *Willing Winnie* snapped at Langar, 18 December 1944 following a tiring trip to Gdynia. On this occasion she was flown by Flg Off Roy Ayrton RAAF and crew, and whose navigator, Sgt Jack Herkes is seen astride her port-inner. Repaired, she later served with Nos 103 and 57 Squadrons before being put out to grass at No 38 MU, Llandow and broken up May 1947. Lewd name and insignia painted on by Cpl Jack Pattison. Where are you Jack? What have you kept to remind you of your handywork which graced so many of No 9's Lancs? *R. J. Harris; J. Herkes*

205

206

207

bomb aimers to accurately set up their bomb sights. A small amount of cloud was drifting across to obscure the target, so the pilot called the force leader on VHF radio for permission to bomb and go home.

As the giant 12,000lb Tallboy bomb was released, the Lancaster seemed to surge upwards into the air. Harris turned and looked down with fascination. It was like giving birth to a huge miniature Zeppelin, which hung suspended for a moment, glistening black in the pale January sunlight, slipped silently beneath them, and was gone.

The Lancaster turned for home, and then came the unexpected escort of German fighters.

The suddenness of the first attack could and should have destroyed them, but the extraordinary impact of the cannon shells gave the pilot a fantastic impetus to execute the 5 Group Corkscrew as he had never done it before. With the first hit, the hydraulics were put out of action. Even as they

207 **Looking Good.** The Harris septet finished their tour on B1 NG499 'WS:W', which, like predecessor PD198, had Merlin 24s driving paddle blade props, and was fitted out for carrying one 12,000lb Tallboy bomb. Ironically, she, two, was scrapped during May 1947 at No 38 MU, Llandow. *C. Allen*

somersaulted through the sky Harris knew this, and he understood what it meant. They were virtually defenceless. The three gun turrets would be quite useless against four fighters, especially in daylight. The only hope was for him to corkscrew again, and again and yet again, while the gunners got in the odd wild shot as the attacking fighters crossed their sights.

The front turret guns were silent. Just before the first attack, Jimmy Parsons had uncoupled his intercom to move forward from the bomb aiming position to his search position in the front turret. Not having heard the recent conversation he was convinced that the plane was crashing. As the Lancaster pulled out of its first diving starboard turn he hurriedly started to remove the bomb aimer's hatch, and prepared to bale out. Only when he turned his head for a last look back did he catch sight of his white-faced skipper mouthing and signalling frantically. He plugged in his intercom.

'Don't leave us yet, Jimmy,' said Harris with a gasp. 'Hold tight' — and the Lancaster rolled into its second corkscrew. When it had finished, Jimmy Parsons climbed up into the front turret. The attacks continued.

Bill Gabriel was in trouble. His rear turret had been hit in the first salvo, and after that he found it almost impossible to bring the guns to bear. His oxygen pipe was severed, and gradually everything started to go pearly grey. Shortly after this he was wounded in the leg, and then above the eye. He nevertheless somehow managed to give evading directions, supported by the mid-upper gunner, whose turret was also useless, while the pilot twisted and turned and flung the heavy Lancaster about the sky. Corkscrew starboard ... corkscrew port ... It was a life and death struggle between the sluggish bomber and the relentless pack of fighters, impossible to throw them off — and nowhere to hide.

Ray Harris was frightened. He had tried every trick he knew, but it was not enough. Several of his crew were hurt, and the constant battery of shells was ripping his Lancaster apart. A fighter flew alongside his port wingtip, and the German pilot grinned across. They were moving in for the kill. He forced the nose of the bomber down towards the sea as another violent explosion flung him from side to side. If he dived low enough he might just throw them off.

The fighters attacked 15 times in all, inflicting such severe damage on the Lancaster that nothing short of a miracle would get it back to England. Only the clear and concise evading directions from the impotent gun turrets and the skilful manoeuvres of the young pilot prevented the Germans from pressing the attacks home. At last, with the Lancaster at 4,000ft, plummeting towards the sea in this last steep dive, the four FW190s each fired a final burst at their erratic quarry, turned steeply away, and set off in a straight file towards Norway. They had travelled to the limits of their fuel, and were heading back to base. The attacks were over.

The problems on board the Lancaster were far from over. The immediate task was to pull the aircraft out of its desperate dive before it was too late. The controls to the trimming tabs had gone, and the pilot realised he could not hold it alone. 'Maurice!' he shouted — 'for Christ's sake give me a hand.' Maurice was the engineer, a big Manchester police-

man. It took all their combined strength to eventually pull the aircraft out. They were at 1,000ft above the sea, having lost 11,000ft since the attacks started. 'Now then,' said Harris, 'let's try and get this wreck home. Is everybody OK?'.

'I need help, Skipper.' It was the first time Bill Gabriel had mentioned his own condition since the attacks started. He sounded very weak. While Ray and Maurice struggled to keep the crippled plane in the sky, Jimmy Parsons helped the wounded rear gunner back to the rest bed. He administered morphine, and tried to stem the blood.

By now the crew was recovering slightly from the shock of this prolonged attack, but they knew they had not won yet. Miraculously three engines were still on full power, with half power from the starboard-outer. The main problem was that the aircraft would stall if the airspeed dropped below 160mph, or if any excessive manoeuvre was made. They must maintain their present height of 1,000ft. Any more stalling and they would be in the sea.

Harris was worrying about landing. He tried the flaps, with no result. Without hydraulics would the compressed air blow the undercarriage down? What they needed was a long runway, and a wide one. 'Give me a course for Carnaby,' he said.

For some minutes there was silence, then the pilot spoke into his VHF. 'Hello Carnaby, hello Carnaby ... this is Rosen William. Am coming in to land. Wounded on board. Stall under 160mph. May not be able to use undercarriage.'

Slowly, very slowly, they lined up for the runway. Fire engines and an ambulance were converging on the spot where they should touch down. The crew crouched low in the recommended safety positions, leaving Harris to nurse the shell-shattered Lancaster back on to an English airfield. It was his moment. There was a wonderfully gratifying solid clunk, and the undercarriage locked smoothly into position, and then they were down. Nobody felt the wheels touch the tarmac. Harris had to shout to the flight engineer: 'You can stop calling the airspeed Doc — we're down'.

It was one of the finest landings Harris ever made, a fine tribute to the skill of the pilot, and a fitting swansong for the weary Lancaster which had taken so much punishment, and had served its crew so faithfully.

While Bill Gabriel was undergoing an emergency operation for removal of shrapnel from his leg (performed in Driffield Hospital by a German prisoner-of-war doctor) that evening, the rest of the crew drank a lot of beer in a small pub in Lissett. There were a few damp bunks the next morning, but nobody complained. When Don Mackintosh arrived in his Lanc to ferry the crew back to Bardney, he looked at the state of *Winnie*, looked at Harris, and silently shook him by the hand.

Both Bill Gabriel and 'Mac', the mid-upper received DFCs for their part in the mission. Ray Harris had won his DFC a few weeks earlier. For getting *Winnie* and her crew back he was recommended for a DSO by his CO, but nothing came of it. Despite the ordeal, the crew continued on ops, with a new 'WS-W' (BI NG499), to bring its tally to a total of 42 by the end of the war in Europe. Surprisingly, *Willing Winnie* (PD198) also survived the war, though her operational days ended with the Bergen trip.

Relief

208-210   Feeling Great! When you were posted to your squadron, fresh from Con Unit, you had yet to develop your stamp of individuality as a crew. You had still to prove your worth as a fighting team. As new boys you had much to learn, so you felt your way, applying all you had been taught, until you had a few ops under your belt and could apply your own theories, quirks, call them what you will. Perhaps *your* crew added a couple of thousand feet to whatever altitude you were supposed to fly at . . . or maybe you came back at deck level whenever possible — even shooting up trains, anything that moved? No? Well, did *your* crew always arrive back first? Someone had to be first and you recall it was generally the same crew. You never did learn how they did it! They turned in just as good a number of aiming points and efficient fuel states as *your* crew so you suppose they understood thermals or simply had a faster Lanc.

Even if not recording a first-back sequence, maybe this vivid threesome featuring No 49 Squadron's 'EA:A' beating up Fiskerton, summer 1944, reminds you of your final trip? It was not always a good thing to know you were on your last. As professional as you had become, you were also tired, that bit jaded, and you dared not become complacent. You kept up your continual drills and watchfulness right up to the time you joined the circuit. Then — and only then — you let go. What a grand feeling it was, knowing it was all over . . . at least for a while! As reserved as you were, you felt the months of pent-up tension suddenly leave you and, with a cry of '—— 'em all', you hammered across the 'drome rattling windows far and wide. It was worth the mild rebuke your CO no doubt later delivered. Was there not a gleam in his eye? You like to believe there was. Did he not understand? Had he not experienced the very same elation? *All: J. A. Edwards*

Once More to Fight and Fly

We have come home,
Dropping gratefully through friendly skies;
And though in tired brains the engines thunder on,
And images of death remain in reddened eyes,
Though nostrils sniff the legacy of oil and sweat,
And legs must learn to cope with solid ground,
We have come home and are at least alive
To mourn our friends, indifferent now to sight,
Or smells, or sound.

Philip A. Nicholson

211 Low and Slow. Is there a more blessed relief than your 'drome's lighting, pallid in the fractured light of dawn, winking at you through the strange washed emptiness of the countryside . . . familiar runways tilting up to meet you as you prepare to join the circuit . . . hearing your squadron calling up one by one, recognising voices despite the distortion. Then it's into the funnel, conscious the deceptive light can impair judgement should you lose your concentration even for an instant. Nav' calling out airspeed . . . everyone so tired . . . aching eyes still searching for fighters. Is Jerry about, following you in? You remember too clearly, one night when you weren't flying, hearing the stutter of machine guns somewhere out there beyond . . . seeing an 88's cannons lace the distant sky . . . looking up in fascinated horror as a fireball dived earthward and seven good men were goners. What a way to go. They were beyond help now . . . as are you beyond the help of others anxiously awaiting you below. Cutting back on the throttles now and gliding. Full flap . . . nose down . . . motors popping and crackling. Not much wind about . . . she wants to float. Ease here down, but you are more weary than you think and all the crew groan as bald tyres kiss the concrete harshly and you wince in tune to the protesting screech of tortured rubber. Rolling now . . . then silence, save for

the whirr of gyros . . . the clump of boots on scuffed metal . . . eager voices.

Is this how *you* remember it? It *was* for Wingco 'Tiny' Ison (boss of No 156 Squadron) till the day he died in 1973. Are you up there with him in 'GT:Q' coming in to touch down at Upwood? *You*, too, forever there at take-off and landing recording the boys on film. How often do you pull out those snaps and reflect . . . remember?
T. E. Ison

211

212 Who Cares if we Bounce? You had flown in lazy circles over the 'drome patiently waiting your turn to land, seemingly for ages, all the crew tired and irritable after a long trip filled with tension, anxiety and dread since you took off all those hours ago. Finally, you are in the funnels, feeling the engineer cut the throttles and gliding in over the road to town and the railway tracks. The runway rises swiftly to meet you and you flash past the caravan with a quick 'whoosh' to touch down . . . only to bounce into the air again, all aboard shouting abuse at the skipper before he pulls the stick back into his stomach and you come down again on all three to roll freely and easily the runway's entire length till you reach the perimeter track. A cameraman with an eye for a picture captures the very moment a No 115 Squadron Lancaster touches down at Witchford, set against an evening sky of unsurpassed majesty, a sun spinning crimson, setting aflame a mountainous billowing barrier of cloud. It is that time of day when the aerodrome becomes a place of warm enchantment, a million miles from the war . . . until the air is again charged with the noise of crackling Merlins, of whining Dodge and Bedford trucks, the murmur of voices . . .
J. N. M. Heffer

212

213   Tired and Grimy Faces. Dortmund is behind you . . . another day riding the flak-ridden skies of Germany is almost history. You are weary, more weary than you care to admit, longing to get your head down and forget this impious war for a few blissful hours. Your head still throbs with engine noise, the sounds of war, but already that spring in your stomach is unwinding. Ever since you climbed out at dispersal, stiff and awkward and tired, there to open a pack of crumpled Churchmans, or maybe groped in your tunic for a battered pipe, the tensions of the past hours began to drain from you. You savoured the moment you shook the stench of war from your lungs and inhaled the delightful odours of the countryside; whether the warm breeze rippling the ripening corn, a damp sliver of wind, or a wash of rain mattered not. It was England . . . and safety. All that remained was interrogation, a drawn out affair, and you had to wait your turn to run through the trip for the benefit of the intelligence officer before you were free to sample the egg and bacon breakfast that was your right. Witness the tired and grimy faces of the two No 115 Squadron skippers here enjoying a mug of tea laced with rum in the interrogation room at Witchford following the 1,000-aircraft daylight on Dortmund, 12 March 1945. It is hoped publication of this revealing study will result in two familiar faces being identified. *L. J. Pearce Collection*

214

100 SQUADRON (2 FLIGHTS)					DATE MOONRISE/MOONSET			100 SQUADRON 2 FLIGHT				
CAPTAIN	A/C	TOOK OFF	LANDED	REMARKS	BLACKOUT FROM. 18 11 TO 07 30			CAPTAIN	A/C	TOOK OFF	LANDED	REMARKS
DAY OP 14TH OCT		DUISBURG		Pff SUPPORTERS	772	TRACK MILES	940	NIGHT OP 14/15 OCT		DUISBURG		
SECTION I					13.00	PETROL LOAD	14.50	SECTION I				
P/O BARKER	A	06 46	11 17	PRIMARY	13×1000 0.025 **BOMB** 12×1000 m.0025			F/O HEALY	B	00 27	05 27	PRIMARY
F/L ROBB	A²	05 25	11 08	"	4×500 LD **LOAD** 4×500 LD			F/O STUART SMITH C 2ND PILOT	M	00 13	05 34	"
F/O HEALY	B	06 34	10 46	"	65140	ALL UP WEIGHT	65327	F/O PARKINSON BASLOW 1ST PILOT	P	00 06	05 52	"
F/O McKENZIE	D	06 26	10 53	"	02 30	NAV MEAL	20 30	F/L BROWN	S	00 05	05 31	"
F/O GRIFFITHS	E	06 21	10 55	"	03 15	NAV TRANSPORT	21 15	F/O HASSLER JACKSON	T	00 15	05 22	"
S/L IRVING	F	06 30	10 51	"	03 30	NAV BRIEFING	21 30	F/O THOMSON SMITH E 2ND PILOT	W	00 11	05 29	"
T/O McVERRY	J	06 53	11 07	"	03 15	OPERATIONAL MEAL	21 15	F/O LENEHAN	X	00 02	05 45	"
F/O GEORGE	K	06 41	11 29	"	04 00	CREWS TO TECHNICAL SITE	22 00	F/O SMITH I G EDLUND 2ND PILOT	Y	00 21	05 58	"
F/O BELL	L	06 29	10 50	"	04 15	MAIN BRIEFING	22 40	SECTION II				
F/O STUART	M	06 40	11 03	REACHED △ Bombs hung up	05 15	CREWS TO AIRCRAFT	23 10	F/L ROBB	A²	00 10	05 41	"
F/O ELLIFF	N	06 24	11 01	PRIMARY	06 15	TAKE OFF	00 05	F/O McKENZIE	D	00 17	05 34	"
F/O PARKINSON	P	06 3	11 10	"	07 13	DEADLINE	01 01	F/O GRIFFITHS WARD 2ND PILOT	E	00 24	05 44	"
F/O EDLUND	Q	06 33	10 56	"		FORM G.		F/O McVERRY	F	00 31	05 48	"
P/O SMITH E M	S	06 23	11 15	"		AIRCRAFT SERVICEABLE.		F/O GEORGE	G	00 19	05 46	"
F/O JACKSON	T	06 35	11 13	"		CREWS OPERATIONALLY FIT.		F/O BELL HOYLE 2ND PILOT	L	00 14	05 26	"
F/O ORDELL	U	06 28	11 11	"		CREWS UNDER TRAINING.		F/O ELLIFF	N	00 18	05 36	"
F/O THOMSON	W	06 29	10 48	"		CREWS ON LEAVE.		P/O HOY	Z	00 20	05 43	"
F/O LENEHAN	X	06 31	10 58	"		CREWS NON-EFFECTIVE.		SECTION III				
F/O LADBURY	Y	06 37	10 42	"		OFFER.		P/O BARKER	A	00 29	06 02	"
F/O HOY	Z	06 32	11 05	"		DERBY.		F/O COPLAND	R	00 23	05 37	"
						GOODWOOD.		F/O ORDELL	U	00 25	05 59	"
						GARDENING.						
						DETAILED.						

214   Two True. Did you ever consider those who stayed behind while you prosecuted the war? Probably little for you centred all your mind and effort on seeing your trip through and getting to bed once it was over. To you, your station intelligence officer, met' man, and others of their ilk appeared as benign, elderly, rather aloof individuals. They and the many others — the erks and WAAFs who manned the telephones, talked you down — you gave little thought to. You accepted they, like you, had a job to do, were just as much a part of the war as you who carried the conflict to the enemy. The nearest you ever got to learning all that went on to support you was when doing your stint as Officer i/c Operations, or, long after your tour was over, serving out your time as an air traffic controller or staff officer at Group. Most of you never found out. When you did your turn in the watch office you endured long hours of anguish, pacing up and down, mentally running through the trip you felt you should be on, all the time willing the fingers of the wall clock to move on to the time when the first hint of engines would herald return of your squadron. Through those long hours of waiting you saw those very men and women you called penguins in a new light and you marvelled at their self-control, their patience. When it was over and the crews had dispersed to their messes and their beds you were left with an operations board telling in chalk and bald facts the story of your station's effort. Too often there would be gaps and the fateful word 'missing' against too many names. Naturally, few pictures were taken of these ops boards, fewer still of life behind the scenes. When the Groupie did call for a camera it was to record an operation notable for its success, as here, displaying No 100 Squadron's contribution to the massive attack on Duisburg by day and night 14-15 October 1944. Through the enterprise of Waltham intelligence officer Flt Lt Bill Lampitt we can see how operations were planned, beginning with the navigators' meal and briefing and working through to take-off. The entry 'deadline' refers to the latest possible take-off for any crew whose aircraft developed last minute problems. Worthy of mention, too, are the track miles, petrol and bomb loads. Note also that all crews attacked the primary target (though one crew's bomb load hung-up), while 'second dickey' pilots were only carried on the night raid. *S. Parkinson*

Return

215-216 Long Wait! You will never forget the warm feeling of satisfaction you felt when you took your turn to bring home the boys newly released from POW camps in Germany and Poland. With hostilities over you needed to be kept busy. Suddenly, life had seemed flat, lacking urgency and purpose. For too long your daily life had been ruled by operations, a recurring round of foreboding and fear, excitement and expectancy, intermingled with leaves home (or in any hotel, rooming house or pub in London if you couldn't make it) . . . vital to keep you going if you were to face the mounting uncertainty which always lay ahead. At first you did not perhaps relish the idea of being used as a taxi service; it had all the makings of being a chore, a total bore, lasting weeks. How wrong could you be! You flew your Lancs to places like Juvincourt and Melsbroek and you hung about for hours waiting for the Tannoy to call your flight number. During that time you marvelled at the patience shown by pathetic groups of soldiers, sailors and airmen waiting to board an endless stream of Lancasters, Stirlings and Dakotas. When finally it was your turn to load-up your hearts went out to the motley collection of gaunt, ill-dressed, ill-fed humanity before you. The flight home was a revelation, too, as, one by one, your passengers took turns to view again old England's shores, talking endlessly and not without dabbing away the odd tear.

(215) Examine the look of bewilderment on the face of this former POW as Sqn Ldr Cyril Hagues from No 15 Squadron, Mildenhall gives a helping hand before they leave Juvincourt in B1 ME455 'LS:O'. (216) Chalked-on inscriptions tell their own story on B1 HK692 'AC:Q' from No 138 Squadron, Tuddenham, also engaged on 'Exodus' May 1945. Inscriptions of a far different kind would be added to HK692's fuselage two years later when she was sold as a 'lot' from No 39 MU, Colerne, and 'reduced to produce', June 1947. ME455 met the same end at No 38 MU, Llandow, some three months later. *P. B. Rosenhain; S. K. Sickelmore*

217-218   Here Today . . . Gone Tomorrow. Suddenly, following weeks of rumours and waiting, endless waiting, the day has arrived . . . you are going home. There is a buzz of excitement in the air, you are eager to see your homeland . . . yet for a long time to come one part of you will remain here on the flat plains of England. For as long as you care to remember your mind has been geared for war; your whole life has revolved around your station, your squadron, your crew . . . and now you face the world outside, a world from which you have become detached while in Air Force blue. Going into town, either as a crew or alone for an evening's jollity, or a weekend '48' in London was merely a tonic. Now you must face the reality of life as a civilian again and you wonder how you will adjust. You will somehow be a stranger in a foreign environment and will surely miss the unique comradeship of service life. Presented here are two views of Croft, 6 June 1945, as the 'Iroquois' and 'Bluenose' Squadrons prepare for their trans-Atlantic return.

(217) We see the Station Commander addressing a huge gathering of station personnel, thanking them for their loyalty and effort, and wishing them well in the years ahead.

(218) No 431 ('Iroquois') Squadron's BX KB807 'SE:B' preparing for take-off, first stop St Mawgan. As with sister units from neighbouring Middleton St George, the Croft squadrons would fly back in stages and this accounts for the immobile Lancs in their dispersals visible in the background. Once back in Canada both the 'Iroquois' and the 'Bluenose' outfits would barely settle into the routine of training for Tiger Force before they would disband at Dartmouth, Nova Scotia, 5 September 1945. KB807 would be handed over to Eastern Air Command and languish in storage until declared surplus as 'war assets' January 1947. *Both M. Bachinski*

218

219   To Forget, You Must First Remember. . . . You are back. The war is behind you and you are again a civilian. The shooting has stopped and the shouting has died down till there is little more than a whisper left. It is time to sit down and relax and forget, but to forget, you must first remember. You miss the flying though you face the prospect of nightmares for years to come — without realising it — and you will never be quite the same again. You wanted to come home, yet hated to leave days filled with a camaraderie you never before knew existed. Days filled with high charges of excitement, with waiting, with boredom, with adventure, with surprise, with happiness and with heartache. And there were the nights . . . long nights that were cold and dark and ridden with fear and protest, and noise and sound and killing; nights that were filled with the stench of death until death became a part of living and was accepted as commonplace as the morning sprint to the ablutions hut. Here, atop the port Merlins of a redundant 6 Group Lanc X at McLeod, Alberta, are on port-inner, Stewart Murphy, formerly with No 431 ('Iroquois') Squadron RCAF, along with Francis Kaye, one-time member of No 426 ('Thunderbird') Squadron RCAF, on port-outer. *J. S. Patterson*

Tears All the Way

*I remember Dortmund, Osterfeld, Cologne,
The probing fire of 88s,
The searing searchlight cone.
I remember Gelsenkirchen, Dusseldorf, Berlin,
The pyrotechnic tracer
And the fighters closing in.
Dessau, Scholven, Bremen, I recollect them well;
We bombed them from the Heavens,
From the ground they gave us hell.
I remember watching
As the sullen bonfires grew,
And with them flowered the bitterness
Of those we never knew;
But now, though man has long rebuilt
These devastated places,
I fancy they are haunted still
By pale forgotten faces;
The shades of those who felt the fear
And lunacy of war;
Who understood its agony
But not what it was for!*

Philip A. Nicholson

Anywhere But Where I am

*The drone of engines irritates
Dry mouthed and taut the crew awaits
The climax each in his own way.
The gunners wet their lips and peer
Nervously into the night, while fear
Creeps up behind like a ghost.*

*We cannot help ourselves, we are
As leaves in Autumn: modern war
Has little room for private fears.
Impersonal, no god of wrath
Compels us, sirens mask our path
And trembling cellars curse and pray.
The tension cracks, a bright cascade
Of colour bursts the night Afraid?
No, more than that, much more than that.*

*The night becomes a madman's mass
Of noise and colour; seconds pass
Like hours. We lurch and help increase
The chaos down below, then leave
All dignity behind and weave
Hurriedly from that horrid place.
The clouds reflect the distant glow
Of shattered houses, streets that flow
With molten tar and frenzied flames.*

*Relax they cannot reach us now
A furtive moon creeps up below
And fills the night with shadows.
Young eyes are dulled and purple patched,
With faces drawn old age is matched
By great fatigue and weariness.*

*At last the engines' final roar
And fumbling fingers seek the door;
The night still surges in our ears;
The night is gone.
Scarlet the East that sets the skies aflame
In angry dawn;
Or does the night withdraw from us in shame?*

Anon

Furrows into Silence

The Lancs have left; from Fenland skies
The clamour and the fret has gone.
Their crews and those who watched with anxious eyes
For homing kites are long departed.
Through roofless huts and fissured tarmac grow
The thrusting weeds
And there is little left to show
What once was here.

220

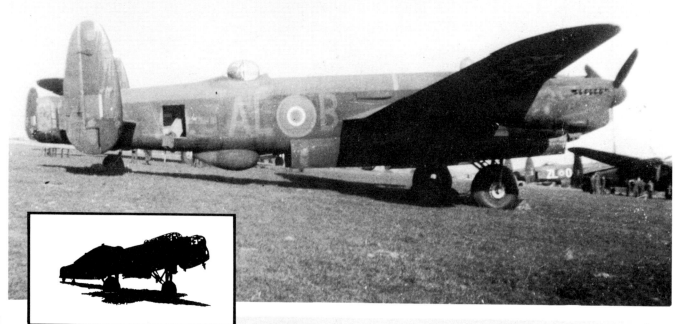

221

220-221 War Surplus. Within weeks of peace being declared in Europe you Canucks, Aussies and Kiwis had booked your tickets home by the hundred. The bars in York and a dozen or more centres of entertainment had echoed to the sound of gaiety and laughter as you got stinko and said your goodbyes in uproarious fashion. That is unless you were in squadrons like Nos 427 ('Lion') and 429 ('Bison'). If you were, you accepted with reluctant resignation the news that you had to stay behind while your fellow 6 Group countrymen headed west. Not for you a crack at the Land Of The Rising Sun as members of Tiger Force. True, you enjoyed the experience of bringing back former prisoners of war, followed by returning British troops from Italy; but you somehow missed the air of expectancy — even the foreboding — which was forever present during operational days. You never settled to a routine day-

to-day flying programme having no real urgency . . . and you *certainly* reacted to all the petty restrictions and rank consciousness which steadily crept in. Those of you far from interested in making the Air Force a career felt only relief when your squadrons closed down.

(220 and 221) Canadian Hal Bowles kept his camera handy when word went round that the Lions and Bisons were to disband at Leeming on 31 May 1946 and fly their Lancs to No 5 MU Kemble for storage and eventual scrapping. Here, 'AL:B' is BIII ME543 of the Bisons, while BIII ME501 is 'ZL:T' from the Lions. Both units had outlived Nos 424 ('Tiger') and 433 ('Porcupine') Squadrons (also transferred to No 1 Group at the end of August 1945) by some seven months. *Both: H. G. Bowles*

146

222 Another Time . . . Another Place. . . . Standing on the same spot some four decades later it is at first difficult to imagine such a wild expanse of open farmland could ever have been an operational two-squadron Lancaster base called Spilsby. Then, quite magically, in your mind's eye you view again the paraphernalia of war. From the Lancasters themselves, seemingly parked untidily at irregular angles around the field, you see again the watch office, solid and dominant, along with its attendant clutch of buildings and vehicles; you pick out the innumerable gantries and gharries and bowsers . . . and, of course, the blue-clad humanity quietly 'oiling the machinery' of Bomber Command. Early morning vista, Spilsby, April 1945, from atop a No 44 (Rhodesia) Squadron Lancaster. The station has yet to come to life; even the windsock is still and lifeless. Few airmen have arrived from their flight offices to remove covers from 44's Lancs and the DIs have barely begun. Note that both top fuselage escape hatches are open. *E. E. Whitehouse*

222

223

223 They Died from Here. For you one-time combatants seeking to retrace your past, and for others of a younger generation wishing to see the bases from whence Bomber Command launched its aerial might . . . beware. Little remains of yesterday's airfields — names typified by Gransden Lodge, East Moor and Methwold — so English — yet seemingly of another world and whose names on signposts at road junctions pointing to villages off the beaten track mean nothing to tourists and holiday-makers hurrying elsewhere. This is Croft, North Yorks, as viewed from an orbiting No 431 ('Iroquois') Squadron RCAF Lancaster and revealing the familiar layout of three runways and with dispersal pans running off the perimeter track. While all aerodromes were built to specific patterns, each had its own distinctive features arising from the need to blend with the surrounding environment such as farms and villages. To you tired crews returning from operations, groping your way through low wrack or swirling fog banks, often in total darkness save for barely visible Drem systems, one 'drome looked like another, of course! Today most have been ploughed up and returned to the land. From ground level inspection you find that few of them bear much resemblance to the once hives of activity, clean-cut expanses of concrete and mass of huts they once were. From the air, even with runways and peri-tracks ripped up you note their shapes and outlines are, however, quite clearly defined and to engage in a cross-country stooge in a Piper or Cessna can be an absorbing experience. You wonder what future aerial archaeologists will make of these enormous scars spread across the landscape! Croft these days is partly farmland, partly a race track and you veterans returning to the haunts of your youth will find little to recognise. Long gone are the hangars and watch office . . . and the warbirds of the Iroquois and Bluenose. *M. Bachinski*

147

224-226 **Ghosts in the Corn.** Do *you* believe in ghosts? Perhaps not, yet, can those of you who have returned to the aerodrome once the centre of your daily life, your very existence, put hand on heart and not admit to having sensed an air of uneasiness, an awareness of the past quite unnerving? As you searched to find a sign of your 'drome's identity, once so alive with humanity and machines at its command, always, at every turn, you found new surprises, new sensations. Everything you had valued and cared for, suddenly was there in the midst of the lonely moors, wild expanse of fenland, wherever yours had been. It was at once rewarding and disappointing. You had expected more and you found so little. Perhaps here a hangar, rusting and given over to storage; there a watch office, long a mere shell but still dominating all before it; but little else, save for the odd lone Nissen (these days looking more like a half-buried tin can than ever before), and crumbling stretches of concrete. As you stood there scanning the emptiness before your gaze, it was as though you were a spectator viewing another world. Even hardened as you were to an every-day world of tensions and pressures of a far different kind, did you not feel a sense of strangeness, a medley of undefined forces closing in on you? Whether your pilgrimage was on a day of fine drizzle, when wisps of grey mist appeared to float above flat and unending vegetation and corn like muslin, or a day of high summer when cotton wool clouds, touched by the sun's glow, drifted across the sky in stately procession, the visions were the same. You were lost in a sea of Lancasters, running-up, queuing at the runway's end, and taking off . . . your head ringing to the sound of Merlins at full stretch . . . to you, as sweet a sound as any composed by the masters of music. And so the visions continued to dance before you until the shadows closed in and the moon swam out from behind tumbling clouds. It was time to say farewell.

Here, a yesteryear witnesses threesome. (224) July 1980 was a glorious month for seeing the 6 Group aerodromes of Yorkshire and Durham. Here, a Skipton-on-Swale at peace, framed by windowless walls of solid brick that still identify the watch office. *M. A. Garbett/M. F. Chandler*

(225) Langar, July 1980, with a T2 hangar steadily shedding its once black corrugated sheeting as the years pass. *B. Goulding*

(226) Serenity, too, as we look across Methwold from the northern perimeter track nine summers earlier. *B. Goulding*

225

226

227-228 Now There are Four. What did you do during the war daddy? Doubtless, at some time or other one of your children asked the question. That was a good many years ago, of course, but even then you found it far from easy to show them a Lancaster if the questioning persisted. Now, when your grandchildren ask the very same question, many of you face a nigh impossible task. If you live in Britain and can take in one of numerous air displays mounted countrywide during summer and autumn, you are in for a treat. It is then you sigh for a Merlin and dab away the odd tear when PA474, 'City of Lincoln', from the Battle of Britain Memorial Flight, Coningsby — to date, sole airworthy specimen of her breed — delights many a gathering, usually in company with the equally legendary Spitfire and Hurricane.

If you must watch the pennies, or your time is short, you can view R5868 — one of only three complete operational Lancs

Lancaster Sunset

Once, those roaring Merlins lifted her,
Laden and eager across sullen seas
And alien skies into agonies of
Fire and conflict; brought her safely
Through a hundred weary homecomings
And anxious touchdowns to survival
And peace.
Now, forty years on, the purpose blunted,
Anger purged, she hauls her ageing
Bones off the ground, flies gentle
Circuits to please the curious and the
Nostalgic and taxies sedately to
Her lone dispersal; there, the
Old eagle, tamed and hooded, to
Await darkness and to dream
Of other far off less untroubled nights.

Philip A. Nicholson

28

surviving — at the RAF Museum, Hendon ... or inspect DV372's nose section in the Imperial War Museum, Lambeth. Further north, there is always NX611 guarding the gates at Scampton, or KB976 at Strathallan ... but more of her later.

Australia has but two, New Zealand one. Journey to Canberra and you find W4783 — another operational veteran — dominating the Australian War Memorial collection, while at Perth, owned by the Air Force Association, resides NX622, which, like NX611 in England, and NX665 at the Museum of Transport and Technology, Auckland, was presented by the French Government following years of service out East.

Canada boasts no fewer than 10 but they are widely scattered, so vast is the country. Five are in Ontario alone. They range from KB944 displayed at the Museum of Science and Technology, Rockcliffe Air Station, Ottawa ... to FM212 pylon-mounted in Windsor's Jackson Park. Check, however, before you move on to Toronto's National Exhibition grounds, for FM104 was last reported in sorrowful condition, despite being on a plinth and thought vandal proof. But take heart when you see the effort put in by dedicated enthusiasts on KB889 at The Age of Flight Museum, Oshawa Airport (reputedly destined for English preservationist Doug Arnold) ... FM213, too, by as keen a band at Hamilton Airport. Alberta has three. FM136 at McCall Field, Calgary is another firmly embedded in a stone plinth at the Centenial Planetarium, while FM159 was last heard of in a roadside park at Nanton, set on blocks and in wheels-down attitude. KB994 is the third, at Westerose, but you'd welcome an up-date for her state and future seems uncertain.

Nothing like the Lanc Xs you knew is KB839 at Greenwood, Nova Scotia. Suffice to say she doesn't look right with that lengthened nose (a postwar mod), though you must admit she's in beautiful condition. Finally, if perchance you find yourself in New Brunswick you might call at St Jaques Airport, Edmunston and ask the local Air Cadet Squadron to show you Canada's one remaining operational Lanc, KB882, in their charge. And that's it, apart from KB848's nose held by the Canadian National Aviation Collection, and a few remnants here and there. You could fill several books recording their chequered histories (R5868, NX611 and PA474 *have* had books written about them), and it needs but a few lines on KB976 to sharpen your resolve to support the next appeal which comes through your letter box.

(227) KB976 was just another Lancaster staging through Debert, Nova Scotia, June/July 1945 when a Canuck photographer snapped No 405 ('Vancouver') Squadron RCAF on its return from service with Bomber Command. Thirty years later you wonder whether he heard about a British Caledonian crew (in command Captain Alec Mackenzie DSO, DFC, one-time two-tour Lanc skipper) flying her from Namao near Edmonton, Alberta, to Strathallan, Perthshire in Scotland, the home of Sir William Roberts' Strathallan Aircraft Collection. Are those who ferried her to the UK in May 1945, and her No 405 Squadron crew who made the return trip weeks later from Linton-on-Ouse to Canada aware, even interested? Need they know she crossed the Atlantic for the third time and touched down at Abbotsinch (Glasgow Airport) 20 May 1975 (228) under the civil guise of G-BCOH), moving to Strathallan 11 June for what appeared at the time to be her final landing? There are now encouraging signs, and how rewarding it will be, if one day she can join PA474 in majestic flight ... KB889 and FM213, too ... perhaps?
N. Malayney Collection; S. Davidson

The Final Word

Sqn Ldr C. S. M. Anderson

Sqn Ldr C. S. M. Anderson RAF, Officer Commanding, Royal Air Force Battle of Britain Memorial Flight, Coningsby.

In his Foreword Sir Harold Martin states that he feels it would be of interest if I could recount my sensations of flying this war winning aircraft. It is a request that is often asked yet is not a simple one to fulfil, as it is impossible for me to separate the aircraft itself from what it represents. I am also acutely conscious that flying the Lancaster today on a sunny Sunday afternoon is a very far cry from operating the aircraft under the conditions for which she was built; furthermore, PA474 is no longer a 'standard Lancaster'.

PA474 is in magnificent fettle, and is in far better condition in many ways than the more modern aircraft with which she now shares a hangar. There is virtually no known corrosion on the airframe, or any other significant signs of fatigue. As far as I am aware there is no foreseen structural end life for the aircraft and it is often said she should be fit to fly in the year 2000 at the present rate. No one has yet refuted that. Some 'original' spares are in short supply and some modifica-

tions have been made to the original specifications to keep her flying: the tailwheel assembly is off a Lincoln; the mainwheels are modified Shackleton wheels and tyres; she has York propellers, and Merlins from whatever.

In order to prolong the airframe life the aircraft is kept as light as possible. All the armour plate and ammunition tanks and tracks have long since gone, whilst the fuel load is normally kept to 1,000gal, and a maximum all-up weight of 47,000lb aimed at. The engines, although not normally operated at more than 2,400rpm and +4lb of boost (except

229   A Tale of Two Cities. If you were fortunate enough to rub shoulders with Lincoln 'Yellow Bellies', and others from afield, gathered together on 25 March 1975, you sensed the feeling of pride as you bore witness to as historic a ceremony as was ever performed. On that fine spring day two cities — as steeped in history as any in a sceptred isle — were linked together in a unique way when PA474 was formally adopted by the City of Lincoln. After all, if a person of distinction can be honoured by a town or city, why not an aeroplane? Long may this 'twinning' between Lancaster and Lincoln continue. *B. Goulding*

229

for take-off, when 3,000 and +7 is used for as short a time as possible) are still capable of producing full 'combat' power if necessary. With that power-to-weight ratio the old lady is quite sprightly and would readily top the imposed 'never exceed' speed of 200kt if asked. Normal cruising speed is around 150 to 170kt at 2,000rpm and zero boost, which uses about 150gal of fuel an hour. Again, to save wear and tear on the airframe the maximum airspeed for operating the undercarriage, flaps, and bomb doors has been reduced to 150kt.

Goodness knows what the Lancaster was stressed for in its operational days, but PA474 is normally kept to less than 1.5G with 1.75G being regarded as a maximum. To achieve this, 30 degrees of bank in turns is seldom exceeded. The aircraft is operated and maintained more or less in line with the Lancaster Manual, although most of the aircrew checks and some of the servicing schedules have been updated in line with Shackleton techniques. As a rule, whenever the aircraft flies she carries a crew of nine: Two pilots, flight engineer, navigator, and five BBMF groundcrew who act as lookouts during flight, and service the Lancaster and her escorting fighters on landing.

In terms of aircraft handling the Lancaster is a delight. In flight she is wonderfully stable and readily flies 'hands off'; the autopilot is no longer fitted. In transit the co-pilot normally does the flying; the captain sits back and monitors progress and thinks about the upcoming display. Although a modern TACAN air navigation aid is fitted, the navigator's art is usually practised by stopwatch, compass, and eyeball, using one quarter inch and one inch-to-the-mile maps. The navigator strives for absolute accuracy of timing for arrival at an air display and is normally within a very few seconds. During the display the captain flies the aircraft to a standard routine, with the co-pilot responsible for all the necessary power changes, the navigator monitoring the display orientation and timing, and the flight engineer the engines, height, and speed. The lookouts keep a keen eye for hazards such as balloons, aerials, and other aircraft. Being such a stable aeroplane and having somewhat heavy ailerons, the Lancaster is physically quite demanding on its pilot during a display sequence. She feels very solid and instils great confidence in the crew.

In her annual flying programme the Lancaster will do some 75 hours and 70 displays, so she works quite hard; and like most aircraft the harder she works, the more serviceable she remains — not that serviceability is usually a problem. If the Lancaster fails to turn up at a display for which she is booked it is normally as a result of the weather. Because of her age and instrumentation she is seldom flown if the cloud base is below 1,500ft and flight visibility less than three miles. We try not to fly in rain as, firstly, the aircraft leaks and secondly, it becomes almost impossible to see out, there being no windscreen wipers. Crosswinds for takeoff and landing are limited to 15kt, and at the start of the season a 10kt limit is self-imposed. For the purist, I have given up trying for a perfect threepoint landing. With the very light wing loading, and a threshold speed of 95kt I find it very difficult to put the aircraft on the ground where and when I want it; hence you

will normally see the old lady 'wheeled' gently on to the runway — probably with a wing down in a crosswind. For me that feels the safest and best technique. 'What sacrilege' I hear some of you say, but it is the one phase of flight which gives me the greatest cause for concern. That is how I deal with it, and for me it works. My successor may well do otherwise.

Every flight in the Lancaster is a great privilege and an immense pleasure which is enjoyed equally by all who fly and service her with much tender loving care. Yes indeed, 'our' Lancaster — or 'yours' if you flew, maintained, or built them during the war — is a much loved aircraft. She has an atmosphere all of her own, and though she never saw active service, represents those that did; long may she continue to do so. I do know that in my opinion those aircrew who flew her sisters during the war were magnificent people. For me, 100ft above the ground during a display is low enough; but the thought of operating at just over half a wing span's height above water at night, let alone without people trying to kill me, makes me cringe. I cannot begin to imagine the sensations of the more routine raids over Germany, nor of operating on the darkest winter's nights. The concept of ferrying a Lancaster all on my own would also be quite a daunting challenge. One can read all the books one likes about flying operations during the war, but we at BBMF are continually humbled by talking to those aircrew and groundcrew who did the job at the time. It is a great honour to meet so many of them through flying the Lancaster.

230

Marshal of the Royal Air Force Sir Arthur T. Harris
Bt, GCB, OBE, AFC, LLD

Air Officer Commanding-in-Chief, Bomber Command
February 1942-September 1945

Born 1892 : Died 1984

Lincoln Cathedral Ahead

Sharp against the black and silver sky
Your bulk looms into view;
The sighting eases tensions, soothes
The creeping irritation of a long trip
And lightens our spirits.
Enduring as the earth itself, symbol
Of the values we cherish, your slumbering power
Renews the strength of those whose
Frailty has been too long exposed
To the buffeting of man and the elements;
And so,
Gratefully we steer our fragile capsule
Into the shadow of your sanctuary;
As also,
The towers of Ely, York and Durham,
Shepherd home our weary comrades.

Philip A. Nicholson

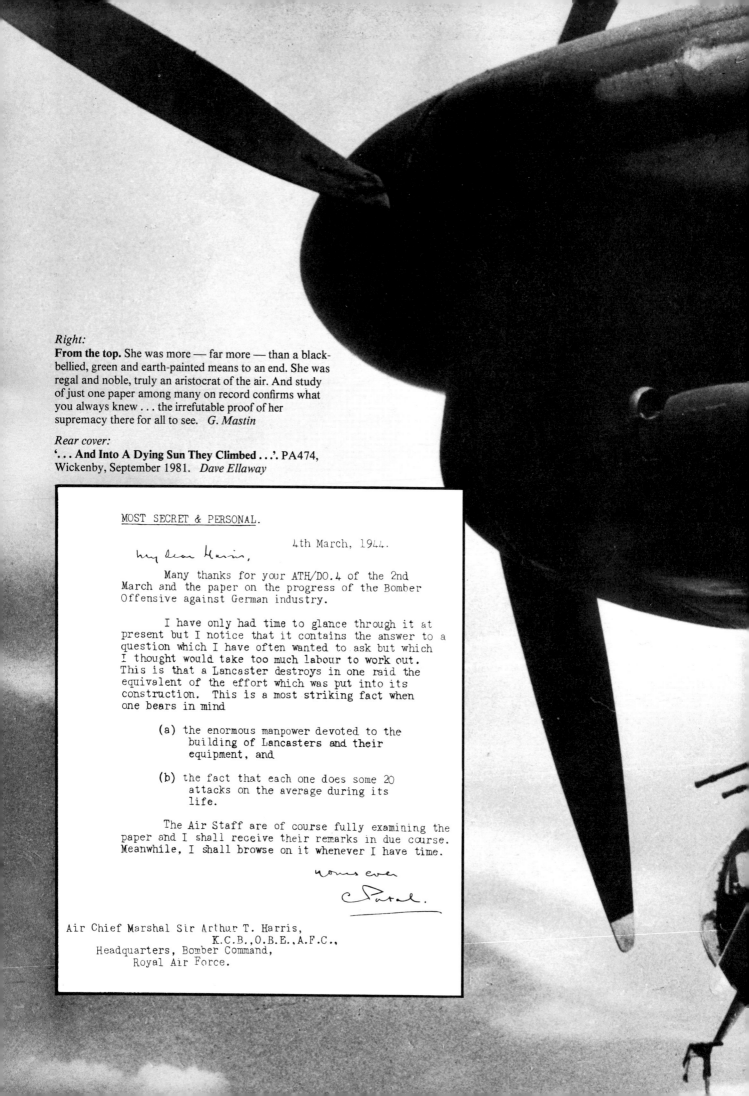

Right:
From the top. She was more — far more — than a black-bellied, green and earth-painted means to an end. She was regal and noble, truly an aristocrat of the air. And study of just one paper among many on record confirms what you always knew . . . the irrefutable proof of her supremacy there for all to see. *G. Mastin*

Rear cover:
'. . . And Into A Dying Sun They Climbed . . .'. PA474, Wickenby, September 1981. *Dave Ellaway*

MOST SECRET & PERSONAL.

4th March, 1944.

My dear Harris,

Many thanks for your ATH/DO.4 of the 2nd March and the paper on the progress of the Bomber Offensive against German industry.

I have only had time to glance through it at present but I notice that it contains the answer to a question which I have often wanted to ask but which I thought would take too much labour to work out. This is that a Lancaster destroys in one raid the equivalent of the effort which was put into its construction. This is a most striking fact when one bears in mind

    (a) the enormous manpower devoted to the building of Lancasters and their equipment, and

    (b) the fact that each one does some 20 attacks on the average during its life.

The Air Staff are of course fully examining the paper and I shall receive their remarks in due course. Meanwhile, I shall browse on it whenever I have time.

Yours ever

C. Portal.

Air Chief Marshal Sir Arthur T. Harris,
                K.C.B.,O.B.E.,A.F.C.,
   Headquarters, Bomber Command,
      Royal Air Force.